POR

Martin Gostelow

Contents

Photo page 1: Cascais
Opposite: Cockerel of Barcelos

This Way Portugal

The Edge of Europe

From the green valleys of the northwest to the golden beaches of the Algarve, Portugal is a land of fascinating monuments and rich traditions. The interior is dotted with picturesque mountain villages and the coast with crusty port towns. Urban renewal may have modernized the capital, Lisbon, yet it is still as quaint as its jolting trams and cobbled streets.

A look at the map shows Portugal as a rough rectangle in the southwest of the Iberian peninsula, taking up only about one-sixth of it, while Spain has the lion's share. About 560 km (350 miles) from north to south and 220 km (140 miles) from east to west, Portugal has a population of just over 10 million.

See the Difference

Portugal packs an astounding variety of scenery into its compact space. The breezy west coast has many fine beaches; resort development there is intended to take the pressure off the Algarve, in the south. The fertile northwest is a land of family farms enclosed by stone walls, pretty valleys and wooded hillsides, while the northeastern frontier is bleaker and wilder, its wide open spaces punctuated by outcrops of granite. Northeast of Lisbon, cattle and horses graze the flat plain of the Ribatejo, the home of Portuguese bullfighting.

South of the Tagus, the gently rolling Alentejo has been a land of great estates and vineyards since the time of the Romans. Wheatfields stretch from horizon to horizon, relieved by a few coppices of cork oak trees with their oddly blackened trunks. A handful of historic cities stand out in the far distance like white ships. Then the mountains, no longer a barrier, that shelter the Algarve with its marvellous coastline and sunny climate.

Land of Explorers

Cut off in the past from the rest of Europe by their sometimes hostile neighbour, the Portuguese turned to their only other frontier, the sea. Their explorers sailed the oceans and returned with riches and tales of the world's wonders. Today, visitors make their own journeys of discovery through Portugal. They find an accessible country, easy to travel in, with a wide choice of charming places to stay. Main highways have been much improved, though the standard of driving remains erratic. 3

Minor rural roads can be rough but the lack of traffic makes the journey a pleasure, as long as you are not in a hurry.

Only the Algarve is in the business of mass tourism, and even there traditional life carries on in the towns and villages. Large parts of the country still see few tourists, rarely enough to affect the local way of life. Lisbon is an exception, though it seems able to absorb the numbers while keeping its distinctive character and style.

Gentle Folk

The Portuguese people are generally modest and courteous, less demonstrative than other Latins. At first, they may not appear forthcoming, though they are friendly and helpful when approached. Ask for directions and you may find someone offering to walk with you to make sure you don't get lost. The musical Portuguese language is difficult to follow—it doesn't sound the way it reads—but English is widely understood, especially in the big cities and by the younger generation. Many speak French, having worked in France (it's said that a million Portuguese live in Paris alone).

Despite mass migration to the cities, most people are still country dwellers at heart and cling to old habits even if they have to live in a high-rise apartment. Balconies are turned into flower gardens, and the courtyards of town houses are filled with fruit trees. It is every family's ambition to own a car, but when they achieve it, the main idea is to drive to the countryside or a beach at the weekend.

PARQUE DAS NAÇÕES

Lisbon seized the chance offered by the EXPO 98 world fair to turn a rundown riverside area east of the city into a bright new satellite. In the biggest project ever initiated in Portugal, abandoned warehouses, docks and an obsolete oil refinery were swept away, and dramatic new structures rose in their place. Unlike some such exhibitions, many of these were designed to be permanent: the largest aquarium in Europe and the "Oceans" Pavilion, for example, in addition to hotels, arts and sports centres, shopping malls and an extension to the Metro. Snaking into the distance is a new bridge, 16 km (10 miles) long, spanning the Tagus and linking eastern Lisbon with new highways to the south. Named in honour of Vasco da Gama, it opened exactly 500 years after he landed on the western coast of India.

Feiras and *festas*, fairs and festivals, are as well attended as ever. Many have their origins in ancient Celtic rituals honouring Mother Nature, long ago adapted into tributes to the Virgin Mary. Most people are Catholic, taking a relaxed attitude to Rome's rules on sex and birth control. The population is actually in decline as a result. The church keeps a fairly low profile; it was deprived of most of its property in the 19th century, and its political influence largely vanished after the 1974 revolution.

POUSADAS

A hotel chain with a difference, Portugal's *pousadas* provide the comfortable rooms you'd expect in the medium to upper price range. Often in out-of-the-way places, their special character comes from the buildings they occupy: medieval castles, convents, a palace or two, or a modest mountain lodge. The most opulent are the equivalent of any top international hotel; others are much simpler and charge less. All of them offer greatly reduced rates in winter. All the *pousadas* have reliable restaurants which feature regional recipes on the menu, and put special emphasis on promoting local wines.

Much-loved national poet Camões lost his right eye during military service in Ceuta.

5

Pace of Change

Not long ago almost everyone depended for a living on farming or fishing. Now only 10 per cent work on the land, and far fewer at sea. Light industry and commerce are the big employers. Women make up half the work force and are taking an increasing role in management. The trend looks likely to continue; over half of all university students are women.

Lisbon can seem like a permanent construction site. Wherever you look, some area of the city is being fenced off or dug up, and the building boom is spreading to other parts of the country. European Union membership has been a big stimulus to the country's economy. As one of the poor-est members, Portugal has benefited from a whole range of grants and subsidies which have brought significant improvements to agriculture and funding for new transport schemes, harbours, dams and tourist facilities.

Big Business

The brightly painted fishing boats on the beaches are not just for show. Fishing is still a vital industry, not only to feed the Portuguese and the tourist legions but also for export. The can of sardines in your kitchen cupboard at home may have originated in Portugal, but for a totally different kettle of fish, try the fresh sardines, grilled outdoors at one of the beachside restaurants.

The big ocean-going trawlers are moored at

the serious fishing ports, like Olhão and Portimão, where the auction of a boatload of fish brings buyers jostling for a look. The captain's livelihood depends on the results, though his leathery face betrays no emotion beyond fatigue. The mariner goes home with a plastic bag in hand, containing a little something he set aside for tonight's fish soup.

Facing the Atlantic brings another advantage. While many Mediterranean beaches are polluted, most of Portugal's are paragons of purity. Dozens have been awarded Blue Flags of approval by the European Union.

Coming Home

In the mid-1970s, when the Portuguese empire finally self-destructed, thousands of colonists returned to the mother country, a place that some of them had never seen. Somehow its less-than-glowing economy absorbed the tide of refugee *retornados*. Many natives of troubled lands such as Mozambique and Angola also fled to Portugal. Thanks to easy-going race relations, some of these, too, have done well, although large numbers live in shanty towns on the outskirts of Lisbon. Africans run market stalls, sell lottery tickets or congregate in and around Rossio square, bringing an exotic note to the street scene. Bands from former west-African colonies add a lively Afro-Latin beat.

Lisbon's famous Ponte 25 de Abril.

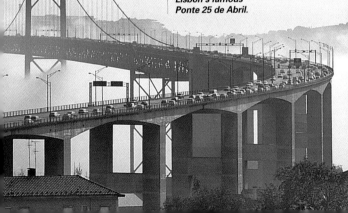

A ALA
DOS
NAMORADOS

Flashback

Early Times

Flint arrowheads and blades scattered over the plains of Portugal show that Stone Age hunters roamed there more than 20,000 years ago. By about 4000 BC, people had settled in communities big enough to build the megalithic monuments that can still be seen: tall standing stones, passage tombs and dolmens (groups of huge stones surmounted by an even bigger capstone).

The Phoenicians, from the distant shores of the eastern Mediterranean, were the first foreign influence. Sailing for the first time beyond the Straits of Gibraltar around 1200 BC, they set up trading posts where ports such as Faro, Lisbon, Nazaré and Aveiro now stand. But they were business travellers, not builders, and left few traces.

Their successors were the Carthaginians, from a former Phoenician colony in North Africa, who ruled the coast until the arrival of the Romans in the 3rd century BC. Meanwhile, tribes of Celts migrating south through western Europe moved into what is now Portugal. They took over the earlier settlements, and built their own fortified hilltop villages, known as *citânias*. Some of these grew into today's towns and cities, and the remains lie buried beneath them. The sites of others, such as Citânia de Briteiros near Braga, have been excavated.

Under the Romans

When the Romans defeated Carthage in the Punic Wars of the 3rd century BC, they quickly seized the Carthaginian colonies and then tried to subdue the interior. It took almost 200 years and the efforts of Julius Caesar, among others, before Celtic resistance was crushed and the peaceful province of Lusitania established.

The impact of the Romans was enormous, and permanent. They introduced the Latin language, the ancestor of modern Portuguese. Roman engineers built roads and bridges, many of which have survived to carry today's juggernauts. Olives and grapes were introduced, and huge areas of the Alentejo were devoted to growing wheat, as they still are.

The Roman legions brought word of a new religion, Christianity, which quickly spread during the 3rd century AD, despite the persecution—and at times martyrdom—of its adherents. By the early 4th century, Emperor Constantine had declared a policy 9 of tolerance, and in AD 330, Christianity became the official state religion. But the empire was in a tailspin by then, and Europe was heading for the Dark Ages.

Tribes from central Europe spread into the Iberian peninsula. Some, notably the Vandals, were intent on looting and destroying, others co-existed with the Romanized inhabitants. The last of this wave of invaders, the Visigoths, arrived early in the 6th century. More disciplined than the rest, they admired Roman ways and adopted a form of Latin; most of them converted to Christianity. Order was re-established for another two centuries.

The Islamic Tide

In the year 711 an invasion fleet crossed the Straits from North Africa, landing a Muslim army in Gibraltar. Led by Arab officers, its soldiers were mostly North African Berbers (known to the Christians as Moors) who came to spread the message of the Prophet Mohammed, to which they were newly converted themselves. Resistance was negligible, and within a few years the Moors controlled almost all of the Iberian peninsula. Although the Christians were able to recapture some northern parts of Portugal before 900, most of the land stayed in Moorish hands for five centuries.

Their legacy—in agriculture, architecture, art, attitudes—can still be seen and felt, especially in the south where they stayed longest. They gave the Algarve its name—in Arabic, Al Gharb means "the west". Towns such as Albufeira, Almansil and Alvor retain their Moorish names to this day, and many a church is built on the site of a former mosque.

Reconquest

The expulsion of the Moors was not the result of one campaign, but an on-again, off-again struggle that lasted centuries. It was hampered by division until the young Afonso Henriques, Count of the northern province of Portucale, seized power from his Spanish-born mother and united the Christian forces. After defeating a small Moorish army at Ourique in 1139, he declared himself King Afonso I of Portugal and set up his court at Coimbra. Lisbon proved too tough a nut to crack until he enlisted the help of some Crusaders, who stopped off on their way to the Holy Land and joined in the siege. After four months, the defenders agreed to surrender, but the Crusaders broke the terms of the truce, looting the city and murdering both Muslims and Christians who had lived under their rule.

Reinforcements from North Africa, the fanatical Almohads,

held back the reconquest of the south for a hundred years, but the Moorish strongholds in the Algarve were eventually picked off. Faro, the last, fell to Afonso III in 1249 and the Islamic presence in Portugal was at an end.

Old Alliance

Energetic kings such as Dinis set about strengthening the new state's defences, building a chain of castles and fortified towns along the border with Castile and Moorish Spain, but independence was threatened when Fernando I died in 1383 leaving only a young daughter. Worse still for Portugal's prospects, she married the king of Castile, who hoped thereby to take over his smaller neighbour. The Portuguese barons rebelled and acclaimed João of Avis, the illegitimate son of Pedro I, as King João I. The Castilian army invaded, but it was routed at Aljubarrota in 1385, with the aid of English archers supplied by John of Gaunt, Duke of Lancaster, who had his own quarrels with Castile.

Thus began the Anglo-Portuguese alliance, often labelled the longest-lasting in Europe. It was sealed by the Treaty of Windsor, and confirmed when Lancaster's daughter Philippa married João I in 1387. Despite interruptions—particularly from 1580 to 1640, when Spain ruled Portugal—and

frosty relations whenever one partner disapproved of the regime of the other, it survived into modern times and remains as something more than a sentimental memory to this day.

Age of Discovery

João I and Philippa of Lancaster had six sons, and among them was the remarkable prince who came to be known as Henry the Navigator. His intellect, imagination and boldness produced one

CAUGHT IN THE MIDDLE

Why did England attack Portugal in the late 16th century, Francis Drake sacking Sagres, the Earl of Essex setting fire to Faro? What happened to the Anglo-Portuguese alliance of 1386? Blame Philip II of Spain, who installed himself on the throne of Portugal when the direct line of succession died out in 1580, and thus dragged Portugal into Spain's war against England. The Faro incident was only a minor foray for Essex, who became a national hero in England when he captured the Spanish bastion of Cádiz. But court intrigues were the death of him. Five years after Faro and Cádiz, Queen Elizabeth had him beheaded for treason.

of history's heroic eras, the Age of Discovery. Though Henry himself never travelled very far, he mobilized an international team of specialists—astronomers, geographers and map-makers, mathematicians and naval architects—and installed them in a sort of think-tank in the Algarve. The traditional site of this College of Navigation is the promontory at Sagres, the windswept "end of the world", although another school of thought puts it at the nearby port of Lagos. Prince Henry convinced his seamen that they could sail into the unknown and return safely in the newly designed caravels. Each expedition out to the islands in the Atlantic and down the coast of Africa went a bit further, bringing back new data to be incorporated on the maps.

By the time the visionary prince died in 1460, his captains had sailed as far south as the "bulge" of west Africa. The momentum continued with the pioneering voyages of Vasco da Gama, who rounded the Cape of Good Hope and founded the colony of Goa in India. Brazil was claimed in 1500, and Portuguese traders soon settled in Sri Lanka, the Moluccas (Spice Islands) in Indonesia and Macau on the coast of China. Portugal presided over the greatest overseas empire of its day.

Dreams and Disasters

Prince Sebastião, born in 1554, was left fatherless at the age of three. He was enthroned as king at the age of 14. Dreaming of a victorious Crusade, he raised an army and sailed from Lagos in 1578, aiming to teach a lesson to the Muslims of North Africa. At Ksar el-Kebir in Morocco, most of his 20,000-strong force was wiped out in the Battle of the Three Kings. The king was reported killed in action; so was his ally, a deposed Arab prince. The Sultan of Morocco, who had been ill, died the next day.

But for many Portuguese, Sebastião wasn't dead, only missing in action; his body was never found. He would return, they believed, and save the country from a power play by Spain. So enticing was the rumour that a series of impostors turned up claiming to be the missing king. It took years for the Portuguese to accept the reality. They still admit to a national weakness for dreams of glory, a syndrome called "Sebastianism".

Sebastião was succeeded by his great-uncle Henrique, but when that elderly bachelor (and cardinal) died two years later in 1580, there was no obvious heir. Philip II of Spain saw his chance to push a dubious claim to the throne, marched in and declared a union of the two nations.

The one-sided nature of the "union" and the arrogance of the Spanish soon had Portugal in a ferment of discontent, but it was 60 years before Spain's grip slackened. A rebellion broke out on December 1, 1640, and shortly afterwards the Duke of Bragança was crowned João IV, celebrated as Restoration Day in commemoration of Portugal's liberation from Spain. As a guarantee of Portugal's independence, the alliance with England was renewed with the marriage of João's daughter Catherine to Charles II.

At Lisbon's historic port of Belém, Henry the Navigator leads the way to new discoveries.

The Worst of Times

Early in the morning of All Saint's Day, 1 November 1755, the earth moved. The earthquake, centred off the Algarve coast near Lagos, was the most terrible disaster of the age. It killed thousands as far away as Lisbon. Churches and castles were razed; fire from church candles which had been lit for All Saints' Day spread to burn down houses; and a tidal wave compounded the devastation. When the dead had been unearthed and reburied and the wounded tended to, the rebuilding began. In most towns, they collected the stones of the old church and put up a new one. Elsewhere, a town square or garden replaced a flattened residential quarter.

The energetic Marquês de Pombal, chief minister to the feeble José I, was in overall charge of reconstruc-

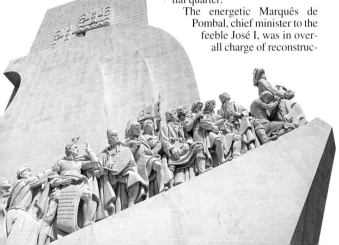

tion. He went on to reform the government, commerce and education but made many enemies in the process. When the Jesuits blamed his "godless" behaviour as the cause of the earthquake, he responded by throwing them out of the country.

Napoleon and Wellington

At the beginning of the 19th century Napoleon put pressure on neutral Portugal to ban British ships, but the Portuguese refused and invoked the old alliance to call for British aid. In 1807 Napoleon lost his patience and sent an invading force under General Junot, prompting the Portuguese royal family to flee to Brazil.

To the rescue came Sir Arthur Wellesley, the future Duke of Wellington, landing with 9,000 British troops north of Lisbon at Figueira da Foz. The French were forced out of the capital, and although Napoleon sent reinforcements and some of his best marshals, they were unable to retake it. At last, in 1811, they pulled out of Portugal with Wellington's army in pursuit. The retreat continued across Spain and into France itself, and Napoleon was forced into exile. When he returned for the "100 days" that led to Waterloo, it was Wellington who was to prove his nemesis. Arguably, by attacking little Portugal eight years before, the French emperor had started the train of events that led to his downfall.

Constitutional Monarchy

British influence in Portuguese affairs continued to be strong, but inspired by the wave of liberalism sweeping neighbouring Spain, a similar movement took hold in Portugal, leading to a constitutionalist revolution in 1820, while the royal family was still in exile. The new constitution was advanced for its time, granting wide individual rights and divesting the clergy and nobility of their privileges. It was accepted by João VI, who returned from Brazil in 1821, but other members of the royal family dissented and a dynastic struggle ensued, pitting

1

THE STRANGEST SIGHT The oldest and weirdest of several such chapels in southern Portugal, the 16th-century **Capela dos Ossos** in the Church of São Francisco in Évora is completely lined with human skulls and bones, dug up from even older graveyards.

liberals against absolutists. After 1834, a shaky constitutional monarchy managed to exist, but as Portugal's finances deteriorated, anti-monarchist sentiment attained fever pitch.

Century of Change

In 1908, as Carlos I and his two sons were riding in a carriage across Lisbon's Terreiro do Paço (now Praça do Comércio), the king and crown prince Luis Felipe were shot dead by assassins. The young prince Manuel was wounded but began a brief reign as Portugal's last king; republican sentiment began to gain ground and two years later he was deposed in a military coup.

The new republic had no easy ride. There were strikes, demonstrations and assassinations, and the trauma of World War I in which Portuguese soldiers served alongside French and British forces on the western front. After the war, the pattern of coups, attempted coups and continual changes of government continued, until a military dictatorship imposed stability. Dr António de Oliveira Salazar, prime minister from 1932 to 1968, organized a degree of economic recovery but neglected other aspects of society. He kept Portugal out of World War II, but his policy of isolation and the cost of military and economic involvement in the colonies turned it into the poorest country in western Europe.

In 1968 a stroke left Salazar incapacitated. His successor, unable to implement sufficient changes to fend off growing discontent, was overthrown in a coup on April 25, 1974—the "Carnation Revolution", a bloodless celebration in which the soldiers carried flowers in the barrels of their rifles.

Years of political and economic turmoil followed, and left-wingers in the army threatened another uprising. But the temperature gradually cooled, with moderate governments succeeding each other in model democratic style. The colonies were given independence one by one, and by 1975 Mozambique, Guinea-Bissau, Cape Verde, São Tomé, Angola and East Timor had all broken ties with Portugal, which absorbed nearly three-quarters of a million refugees, now representing close to 7 per cent of the population. In 1986 the new Portugal was admitted to the European Community (now the EU), which underwrote many new projects, from highways to the renovation of the fishing fleet. Isolated on the very edge of Europe, Portugal used to look to its overseas empire, but that was given up in the rush of revolutionary fervour in the 1970s; now Europe beckons instead.

On the Scene

Portugal's different regions offer a wonderful range of landscapes, historic towns, charming villages and varied customs. The main roads have been greatly improved in recent years, making it possible to cover quite a lot of ground, even during a short stay. This guide begins with Lisbon and excursions from the capital. It then moves clockwise round the country, taking in Oporto, the green northwest, the mountains of the northeast and the great plain of the Alentejo, with its scattered fortresses and palaces, and ends with the holiday playground of the Algarve.

▶ LISBON

Old City and Alfama, Baixa, Bairro Alto,
Avenida da Liberdade, Belém, Major Museums

Lisbon spreads along the slopes facing south across the River Tagus—the Tejo in Portuguese. The city's hills offer magnificent views. It is never overwhelming or grandiose, but there are some striking historic monuments, unique architecture, a handful of notable museums and a wealth of quirky curiosities.

Since the 1980s Lisbon has also acquired all the facilities of a contemporary city—from post-

modern shopping complexes to a Metro system tunnelling beneath the traffic jams. But this transformation has largely been achieved by expanding suburbs or adding new ones, while preserving the character of the old districts. They are still like separate villages, each with its own distinctive flavour.

Within each district, the sights are close enough together to walk from one to another. Buses, taxis, trams and the Metro underground make it easy to move around the city. Parking problems and traffic jams mean that, except on Sundays, a car is a liability.

The trams of line 28 rattle right past the front door of Lisbon's cathedral.

Old City and Alfama

Lisbon probably began as a fishing settlement on the banks of the Tagus, but the need for defences dictated a move to a fortified hilltop. It may have been the Carthaginians who chose the site, now occupied by the Castelo de São Jorge, whose ramparts tower above the east side of the Baixa. The city gradually spread down the hill towards the river, creating the Alfama district. After the Reconquest, it expanded west to the slopes where the cathedral now stands.

The Alfama, the oldest part of Lisbon, lies south of the Castelo de São Jorge, on the slopes above the River Tagus. This was the heart of the Moorish city, and although it has suffered from fires and earthquakes it still has the look of a North African kasbah, a labyrinth of narrow streets shaded by whitewashed houses leaning at odd angles. This medieval street plan—or lack of a plan—adds to the charm of the Alfama district. You're bound to get lost, but the sights and sounds along the way are well worth the trouble. Some streets are so steep they are stepped, others so narrow you have to walk in single file. Decaying mansions with artistic decorations and dilapidated tenements line the streets and squares. Amid the jumble are churches markets, bars and restaurants.

Castelo de São Jorge

The Moors built a citadel where a Roman fort had stood, and stayed more than four centuries. They strengthened the walls to withstand earthquakes and sieges; in 1147 they held out for months before being forced to surrender to Afonso I and his Crusader allies. After the Reconquest, the castle became a royal palace, but it was extensively damaged in the quake of 1755 and fell into disuse. Renovated in 1938, it now features a multi-media exhibition, Olissipónia, and encloses a pleasant park inhabited by peacocks and other exhibitionist birds. There are fine views of the city from the ramparts. Opposite is the Bairro Alto; downriver in the distance are Belém and a suspension bridge, Ponte 25 de Abril.

Viewpoints

Just below the castle, Largo das Portas do Sol is like a balcony over the Alfama. Further down is the Miradouro de Santa Luzia, where you will see two striking panels of *azulejos*. One depicts the expulsion of the Moors from Lisbon in 1147; the other shows how the waterfront looked before the great earthquake of 1755.

Sé

Lisbon's hillside cathedral is embraced by the city; trams clang past the front door, and taxi brakes squeal. Its fortified façade and arrow slits indicate the dangers that surrounded the church in the 12th century when it was begun. Earthquakes battered the building in the 14th, 16th and 18th centuries, giving generations of architects the chance to add to its Romanesque and Gothic beginnings. The sacristy's museum of religious art includes the relics of St Vincent.

St Anthony of Padua, friend of the poor and Lisbon's favourite saint, was born just down the street from the cathedral in 1195. His birthplace is marked by the church of Santo António da Sé.

São Vicente de Fora

East of the Castelo de São Jorge, the twin white towers of the 16th-century church of São Vicente de Fora make a useful landmark. The austere Renaissance look of the exterior continues inside, but there's a surprise awaiting you. The adjoining cloister is brightened by blue-and-white *azulejos* illustrating some of La Fontaine's fables.

A chapel near the cloister contains the tombs of many kings and queens of the Bragança dynasty, from João IV, the first, to Manuel II, the last. Queen Catherine, daughter of João IV and the wife of Charles II of England, is also buried here; she returned home to Lisbon after his death.

Campo de Santa Clara

A flea market, Feira da Ladra, fills Campo de Santa Clara, the open space behind São Vicente, every Tuesday and Saturday morning. As well as selling food and clothing, this "Thieves' Market" is well known for the amazing range of second-hand goods, bric-a-brac and junk spread out on the stalls and heaped upon the ground. You'll marvel at the optimism of the vendors in expecting you to buy some of their dusty rubbish, and the high prices they quote for anything genuinely old or remotely desirable.

Pantheon de Santa Engrácia

Downhill from the marketplace, a white dome rather like a smaller version of the US Capitol tops a building that took three centuries to complete. It started as a church, but was finished in 1966 as a tribute to Portugal's national heroes, including Henry the Navigator, Camões and Vasco da Gama, honoured with symbolic tombs—they are buried elsewhere. It also serves as the actual burial place of Portugal's presidents.

Baixa

Next to the Tagus in the heart of the city, the historic Praça do Comércio (Commerce Square) is now one big car park, surrounded on three sides by graceful arcades. The fourth side is open to the river, with Venetian-style steps down to the water and a ceaseless traffic of ferry boats coming and going.

Around the Rossio

Through a triumphal arch you enter the Baixa (lowland) district, a grid of shopping streets lined with buildings of uniform height. When this part of town was wiped out by the quake of 1755, the bold reconstruction plan was decreed by the Marquês de Pombal, who put Lisbon back on its feet—the rebuilt Baixa was designed to be earthquake-proof. Its chief south–north artery, Rua Augusta, leads to Lisbon's main square—Praça Dom Pedro IV, more popularly known as the Rossio—once the venue for public executions and bullfights. Now, with the adjoining Praça da Figueira, it's the ever-busy terminus for buses and taxis, and the home of outdoor cafés and flower stalls.

At the top (north) end of Rossio stands the National Theatre. Facing it, the strange-looking building with inverted horseshoe archways is the Rossio railway station which serves Sintra.

Bairro Alto

By day, it's always pleasant to stroll through the Bairro Alto along streets of faded but still elegant houses, many faced with patterned *azulejo* tiles. At night, the scene is transformed as bars, clubs and restaurants open their doors.

Elevador de Santa Justa

From the Baixa a free-standing lift climbs 30 m (100 ft) to the Bairro Alto, the "high neighbourhood", noted for its nightlife, as earthy or sophisticated as you like. Inaugurated in 1902, the lift was steam-operated until electric power was perfected. Tour guides usually attribute its construction to Gustave Eiffel, the engineer of the Parisian tower fame, but it was in fact designed by Raoul Mesnier de Ponsard, Eiffel's apprentice.

Another way to reach the top is to take a funicular tram (or walk up the steps beside it) from Praça dos Restauradores, near the Rossio station.

Igreja do Carmo

Near the top of the Santa Justa lift, the 14th-century Carmelite church is the ultimate monument to the great Lisbon earthquake. On All Saints' Day in 1755, when the church was crammed with worshippers, the roof fell in, and that's the way it stands today, Gothic arches open to the sky.

A small archaeological museum on the premises features Roman sculpture, early tombs and even some ancient mummies.

Rossio railway station, in a 19th-century architectural style known as neo-Manueline.

Chiado

The long way back down to Baixa is by the winding roads of the Chiado district, the scene of a disastrous fire in 1988. It wiped out the city's most fashionable shopping area, including two high-class department stores and countless antique shops. Hence the new look, the result of a ten-year reconstruction project.

São Roque

Just down the street from the top of the funicular (Elevador da Gloria), the church of São Roque may not look very impressive from the outside, but the interior is covered with gold, silver, pre-cious stone and marble. It was ordered from Italy in 1742 by João V, at a time when the royal treasury was well funded by the riches of Brazil.

Avenida da Liberdade

Near the top end of Rossio square, behind the Teatro Nacional, the big open space of Praça dos Restauradores commemorates the War of Restoration in which the Portuguese threw out the Spanish in 1640. Lisbon's main tourist information office is housed in the splendidly restored Palácio Foz, facing the square.

From here, the broad tree-lined Avenida da Liberdade heads uphill, ending at a big traffic round-about. Officially Praça Marquês de Pombal, with a statue of the dictatorial aristocrat accompanied by a lion, it's almost always called the Rotunda.

Parque Eduardo VII

Above the Rotunda, continuing in the direction of the Avenida da Liberdade, the park was named after Britain's Edward VII, following a visit in 1902. In its northwest corner, the Estufa Fria (literally "cold greenhouse") is a collection of tropical, subtropical and local plants, trees and flowering shrubs, nurtured in suitable glasshouses, shelters and the open air.

To the north of the park is the first-rate Gulbenkian Museum in its fine modern building.

Aqueduto das Aguas Livres

To the northwest, what at first glance appears to be a Roman aqueduct is in fact an 18th-century water supply system that still serves Lisbon. The long line of tall arches was finished in 1748, just seven years before the fateful earthquake knocked down practically everything in sight. It survived unscathed.

Belém

When the great explorers left Lisbon on the way to their destinies, this is where their voyages began.

Belém, which means Bethlehem, is the historic part of the port about 6 km (4 miles) downstream from central Lisbon. The most atmospheric way to get there, if not the quickest, is by tram from Praça do Comércio.

Padrão dos Descobrimentos

A prominent landmark on the waterfront is the modern Monument to the Discoveries, dominated by a statue of Henry the Navigator holding a model of a caravel, leading a crowd of scholars, mariners and clerics. Near the base of the monument, a map of the world inlaid in the pavement notes the dates and remarkable extent of Portugal's discoveries and overseas settlements.

Museu de Arte Popular

The nearby Museum of Popular Art surveys the folk art, crafts and customs of all the regions of Portugal, with displays of costumes, embroidery, jewellery, furniture and toys.

On the landward side is the big new cultural complex, a convention centre and theatre.

Torre de Belém

Just a short way downstream from the Monument to the Discoveries, the Tower of Belém is an elegant little riverside fortress built early in the 16th century. It's a wonder of stone-carving and the only building to be both started and finished entirely in the Manueline style, a variant of Late Gothic which flourished under the reign of Manuel I. In those days it stood some way out in the river, but land reclamation has brought the shoreline close enough to be joined to the tower by a short footbridge.

Ponte 25 de Abril

The suspension bridge soaring across the Tagus River was built in 1966. At that time the longest in Europe, it was originally named after the dictator Salazar, but after the 1974 revolution it was given the present name, marking the date of that event. On the south bank, high above the bridge's toll booths, the statue of Christ the King *(Cristo Rei)* is a smaller version of Rio de Janeiro's. Beyond the bridge the great river widens out on the last leg of its journey from the mountains of Spain to the Atlantic.

Mosteiro dos Jerónimos

The sprawling Jerónimos Monastery, paid for with profits from the spice trade, is a triumph of the Manueline style of architecture. The long south façade is quite plain, but the doorways are a mass of intricate detail and exotic

Exquisite Belém tower was a welcome landmark for sailors returning home.

decorations evoking the sea and faraway places. Among the kings and heroes buried in the spacious church is the explorer Vasco da Gama, who sailed round the Cape of Good Hope opening the route to India. Opposite his tomb is that of the national poet, Luis de Camões, though it probably doesn't contain any of his remains—the original grave was lost in the 1755 earthquake.

Behind the church, on the north side, don't miss the two-storey cloisters, whose arches are partly filled-in with magnificent Manueline stone-carving. The upper level leads into a gallery inside the church, where you can get a better view of the soaring roof and its supporting columns.

Archaeological and Naval museums

On the west side of the Jerónimos complex, the convent buildings were badly damaged in 1755. Reconstructed in matching style, they now house two museums.

The Museu Nacional de Arqueologia boasts fine collections of Bronze Age and Stone Age jewellery and artefacts, together with some superb Roman sculpture and mosaics.

The Museu da Marinha displays countless detailed models of historic ships, many of them made at the same time as the full-sized versions. In a pavilion facing the museum are original royal barges from the 18th century; each one required 80 oarsmen.

Museu Nacional dos Coches

Towards the centre of Lisbon from the former riding school of the Palacio de Belém, now the home of a collection of horse-drawn carriages, arguably the finest in Europe. From rugged closed coaches for long journeys across rough tracks to gilded fantasies for ceremonial use, they span three centuries of history.

Major Museums

Various unique and unusual collections scattered around the city can be visited when you are in the vicinity, notably the Museum of Coaches, the Naval and Archaeological Museums in Belém. The three star museums listed below are some way from other attractions but well worth a special trip.

Gulbenkian Museum

Armenian-born billionaire Calouste Gulbenkian, who died in Lisbon in 1955, endowed this splendid museum, one of many bequests to his adopted country and not to be missed. On show are some of the thousands of works that Gulbenkian acquired for his private collection, ranging from ancient Egyptian statues to Art Nouveau.

The museum is excellent in many departments, from Islamic art to Chinese porcelain to the paintings by Europe's great masters including Rubens, Rembrandt, Francesco Guardi and Turner. Gulbenkian collected the work of the 19th-century English pre-Raphaelite painters before they came into fashion, so there is a good selection in the museum. And one room contains scores of pieces of jewellery and glass by René Lalique (1860–1945), a friend of Gulbenkian. Across a sculpture garden, the Centro de Arte Moderna presents a survey of 20th-century Portuguese art.

Museu Nacional de Arte Antiga

The National Museum of Ancient Art occupies the 17th-century palace of the Counts of Alvor on a hill above the docks, about halfway between Praça do Comércio and Belém. Among a wealth of paintings, gold, silver and glass, and treasures from the former colonies, look out for three star attractions. First, *The Adoration of St Vincent*, six large panels painted by the 15th-century Portuguese master Nuno Gonçalves show such figures as Henry the Navigator, along with clerics, businessmen and fishermen. It's a remarkable portrait of Portuguese society at the time of the great discoveries.

Dürer and Cranach are represented in the German Art section, but the outstanding exhibit is the nightmarish triptych by Hieronymus Bosch, *Temptations of St Anthony*, dated around 1500.

Finally, five Japanese folding screens painted in the 16th century record the astonishment of the locals at the arrival of Portuguese missionaries and traders. The Japanese had never before encountered black-robed Christian priests, buttons, or big European noses.

Museu do Azulejo

The Convento da Madre de Deus is the setting for a superb collection of historic *azulejos*, ceramic tiles. It stands about 3 km (2 miles) northeast of Praça do Comércio, just inland from the waterfront.

The convent's baroque church, rebuilt after the 1755 earthquake, is rich with blue-and-white tiles from Delft in Holland, but the adjoining buildings contain displays of the whole history of *azulejos* from Portugal: early arabesque, floral designs, religious scenes and large narrative panels. The *Great Lisbon Panorama*, 36 m (118 ft) long, shows the city as it was before the earthquake. A little restaurant operates in the old convent kitchen, itself lined with original tiles depicting all sorts of fascinating food. 25

EXCURSIONS FROM LISBON

South of the Tagus, Costa do Estoril,
Sintra, Mafra, Ericeira

The region close to the capital, north and south of the Tagus, is sometimes labelled Costa de Lisboa. But its attractions are by no means confined to the coast, witness the palaces of Queluz and the old hill resort of Sintra, whose praises were sung by Byron.

South of the Tagus

The best beach near Lisbon is Costa da Caparica on the Atlantic coast of the Arrábida Peninsula. The northern end is lined with apartments used by people from Lisbon, and a little railway shuttles sunseekers along a huge arc of sand to the south.

Serra da Arrábida is a miniature mountain range—and a nature park—along the southern shore of the peninsula. The old fishing port of Sesimbra has turned into a small resort, spread around a bay with the walls of a Moorish citadel on the hill above.

Setúbal

A hard-working port with a big fishing fleet, Setúbal was an important Roman town. The old

Mafra's magnificent marble-clad monastery was built with wealth from Brazil.

fish-salting tanks can be seen through glass panels in the floors of the regional tourist office. The Igreja de Jesus, dating from about 1494, was designed by the French architect Boitac who later worked on the Jerónimos monastery in Belém. Its stone columns, carved like twisted rope, were the first hint of the Manueline style. The town museum next to the church has some fine early Portuguese paintings, panels from its 16th century altarpiece.

Two castles in the vicinity have been adapted as *pousadas*: the coastal Fortress of São Filipe just west of Setúbal and the hill-top castle at Palmela, 6 km (4 miles) to the north.

Tróia Peninsula

A short ferry trip across the wide River Sado from Setúbal lies an 18-km (11-mile) finger of sand, with beaches all the way along its Atlantic shore. Torralta is a big leisure resort at the northern end, with apartment blocks, supermarkets and discos which come alive in summer and stand largely empty for the rest of the year.

Facing the sheltered estuary is the site of the Roman port of Cetóbriga, abandoned in about the 5th century after it had silted up. To find it, head south along the peninsula for 3 km (2 miles) and take the track signposted *Ruinas Romanas*. The ruins include large fish-salting tanks, baths with traces of mosaic and the foundations of port buildings.

Alcácer do Sal

A little old river port on the Sado, upstream from Setúbal, seems to have been bypassed by traffic and modern times. The name comes from Al Ksar, Arabic for fortress, and Sal (salt) reflecting its main product in past centuries. White houses with red tiled roofs cluster on one side of the river below the castle (now a *pousada*), worth climbing up to for the views and the Romanesque castle church of Santa Maria.

In the centre of town is the beautiful Espírito Santo church, now an archaeological museum. A Roman stone-carving seems to show a bullfighter on horseback, suggesting ancient origins for this Iberian ritual.

Costa do Estoril

A half-hour's train ride or a hectic drive along the coast road west of Lisbon leads to the old-established resorts on the northern side of the Tagus estuary. First fishing villages, then winter havens and retirement homes for the well-heeled, Estoril and Cascais now attract visitors year-round.

Estoril

The elegant if faded resort of Estoril has a name as the haunt of the retired rich, led in the past by the exiled monarchs of half a dozen European nations. Now its modern casino is a magnet for gamblers; it also offers golf and hosts the Formula One Portuguese Grand Prix. Crowds from the capital flock to the beach, although the sea can be polluted this close to the Tagus estuary.

Cascais

To the west and almost adjoining Estoril, Cascais is a less formal holiday town which retains some of the feel of the fishing village it once was. Boats are hauled up on the beach, and the catch is taken to be sold in the new auction building. You'll see plenty of swimmers, but to be sure of clean water you need to head west and "turn the corner" to Guincho, where the Atlantic rollers attract hordes of windsurfers. But take care; when it's rough the sea there is only for the experts.

Queluz

West of Lisbon and inland from Estoril stands a pink rococo palace built in the mid-18th century and used by the unfortunate Queen Maria I, who suffered from severe depression after her son José died from smallpox, and who ultimately became insane.

Room after elaborate room is fitted out with giant chandeliers and shabby furniture. The rambling gardens feature a river running through canals tiled with painted *azulejos*, where royal guests took boat rides or staged mock sea battles. The old kitchens have been turned into an unusual restaurant, the Cozinha Velha, run by the *pousada* chain, which also operates a hotel in another historic building nearby.

Sintra

Hailed by poets as a paradise, Sintra is set among wooded hills of the Serra de Sintra, about 25 km (16 miles) northwest of Lisbon. It was the summer home of Moorish rulers and Portuguese kings, and later of eccentrics from all over Europe whose mansions, pavilions and botanical gardens spread across the slopes. The old town grew up around the rambling Palácio Nacional; high above it are the ramparts of a Moorish castle and a bizarre fantasy fortress. Lower down, the village of São Pedro de Sintra holds a famous country market on the 2nd and 4th Sunday of each month.

Palácio Nacional

Two great conical chimneys are the most prominent features of the former royal palace, begun in the 14th century and continually

extended. The outside is hardly beautiful, but the interior is a succession of salons, halls, staircases and bedchambers in a fascinating mixture of styles. The bath houses, inspired by Moorish designs, are lined with some of Portugal's earliest and most valuable *azulejos*.

Guides have a story to tell about every room. In one, the floor is badly worn, supposedly by the pacing of the deposed Afonso VI who was imprisoned here by his brother Pedro II for nine years. The Sala das Pegas has a ceiling painted with magpies, their mouths sealed with the motto *Por Bem* ("in a good cause"), intended as a rebuke to ladies-in-waiting for their idle chatter; the words are those of João I when caught kissing one of their number.

Palácio da Pena

The highest pinnacle in the area, 450 m (1,500 ft) up, is topped by a multi-coloured fairytale folly built in the mid-19th century on the ruins of an old monastery. A romantic retreat for Maria II and her husband Ferdinand, its rooms are decorated in imitation Moorish, Gothic Revival and a wild mixture of other architectural styles, and packed with "Victorian" bric-a-brac—the couple were admirers and close relations of the British royal family.

29

Cork Convent

At the bottom of the steep road down from the Palácio da Pena, a sign to the *Convento dos Capuchos* leads to an abandoned Franciscan monastery. A few low, dark chambers cut into the rock are lined with sheets of cork, which would at least have made the grim little cells warmer. Lord Byron mocked the inmates of the "Cork Convent" for making this life a misery in the uncertain hope of paradise in the next.

Quinta de Monserrate

Fleeing a scandal in England in the 1790s, the eccentric William Beckford bought an estate west of Sintra and built a famous but now-vanished mansion (its landscaped gardens were immortalized in Byron's *Childe Harold's Pilgrimage*). Then a London textile merchant, Sir Francis Cook, spent a fortune on a Moghul fantasy of a palace, sadly empty and neglected today, and a subtropical garden on the hillside.

Mafra

With gold pouring in from Portugal's colony of Brazil, João V decided to mark the birth of a son and heir by building a vast monastery and palace at Mafra, 40 km (25 miles) northwest of Lisbon. It was begun in 1717, with up to 50,000 workers employed. Huge quantities of coloured marble from the local quarries went into the massive basilica, and the total length of the complex, 220 m (over 700 ft) is even greater than Spain's Escorial. The king ordered a 114-bell carillon from the best Flemish bell-founders; it is still in good order and concerts are given in the late afternoon two or three days a week.

The convent hospital was so arranged that the patients in the private sickrooms could see and hear Mass in the adjoining chapel without having to leave their beds. Its pharmacy still has a collection of crude-looking surgeon's tools. Perhaps the highlight of Mafra is the vaulted, gilded library, much larger than the one at Coimbra which dates from the same era.

Ericeira

A pretty fishing village 10 km (6 miles) west of Mafra has become quite a trendy place for Lisboêtas to have a holiday home, so the old centre of whitewashed houses has been ringed by apartment blocks. Ericeira had its moment in history when the last Portuguese monarch Manuel II sailed with his family into exile in 1910, fleeing the revolution. Today its fish restaurants attract diners from the capital and tourists for a lunch break during their excursions to Mafra and Nazaré further up the coast.

◀ COSTA DE PRATA
Peniche, Óbidos, Nazaré, Alcobaça, Batalha, Fátima, Tomar, Coimbra, Figueira da Foz, Aveiro

The "Silver Coast" between Lisbon and Oporto offers several beach resorts popular with local people and Spanish visitors. Inland are some of Portugal's greatest historical monuments: walled towns, medieval abbeys and the former capital and university city of Coimbra. Military campaign buffs come to see the sites of some of Wellington's battles, and to look for traces of the Lines of Torres Vedras, the defence system which he ordered to be built to shield Lisbon from the French.

Peniche
A defensive wall built by the Spanish in the 16th century cuts right across the sandy spit of land that joins Peniche to the mainland. Restaurants line the quay next to the busy fishing port, and the beaches north and south are popular with local families in summer. Holiday accommodation is mainly in small apartments and private homes.

An hour away by ferry, the offshore island of Berlenga Grande is a sanctuary for seabirds.

Óbidos
Completely enclosed by its high walls, the little town of Óbidos is one of the prettiest sights in Portugal—and one of the most visited; arrive early if possible to avoid the crowds. Entering by the tiled southern portal, Porta da Vila, or by the north gate next to the castle (now a *pousada*), you stroll along its narrow streets, between whitewashed, red-roofed houses adorned with masses of bright flowers. The battlements are accessible in places for a better view. It is hard to believe now, but this was a port centuries ago until the bay silted up in the 16th century and the sea retreated out of sight.

Igreja de Santa Maria
Facing the main square, the parish church has some fine 17th-century *azulejos* and an unusual blue ceiling. In a chapel beside the altar, paintings of the life of St Catherine are the work of Josefa d'Ayala, one of the first women to be accepted as a professional artist. Usually known in Portugal as Josefa de Óbidos, she was born in Spain, came to live in Óbidos and died here in 1684.

Museu de Óbidos
Across the square from the church is the 16th-century town hall, now converted into a museum funded by the Gulbenkian Foundation. 31

On three floors including the basement, its collections include relics of the 1808–14 Peninsular War, with maps and weapons similar to those used by Wellington and his troops.

Nazaré

Once there was just a fishing village here, where the flat-bottomed boats were hauled ashore by oxen onto the sandy beach. Now it has been hemmed in by holiday apartments, and most of the fishermen operate from a new port to the south. Some of the charm survives: on special occasions the men wear their traditional stocking caps and plaid trousers, the women their black shawls, embroidered aprons and, it's said, seven petticoats. This is a cheerful, breezy resort: in summer the beach sprouts row after row of sheltering tents.

Sítio

Until the 19th century, the people of Nazaré lived up on the cliff above the north end of the beach, somewhat safer from the ever-present danger of pirate raids. These days, with its own restaurants, holiday accommodation and great views, Sítio is a quieter alternative to Nazaré.

Lavish sculpture adorns the oratory of the Knights Templar at Tomar.

Alcobaça

The largest church in Portugal, and one of its finest medieval monuments, the Mosteiro de Santa Maria in Alcobaça was built to mark a military victory. In 1147, the forces of Afonso Henriques took Santarém from the Moors in a surprise attack, and in gratitude he vowed to establish a Cistercian monastery. The main church was finished by about 1220, in French Gothic style, with a soaring nave 110 m (360 ft) long.

Over the centuries the church was filled with Manueline, baroque and rococo additions. In a controversial attempt to return to the pure original lines, these have all been removed, leaving the stone interior almost bare. In the transept, all the more impressive amid the austerity, is the 14th-century tomb of Pedro I facing that of his beloved Inês de Castro, so that on the Day of Judgement their first sight would be of each other. Each tomb bears the inscription *Até ao fim do mundo* ("Until the end of the world"), and they are embellished with intricate, delicate carvings of biblical scenes; the damage you can see was inflicted in 1810 by pillaging French soldiers.

Adjoining the church are fine two-storey cloisters and the elegant chapter house, with carved figures of saints. Upstairs is one of the monks' dormitories, with 20 columns supporting a magnificent vaulted ceiling. The huge kitchen has a very practical water supply and waste disposal system—a specially diverted stream runs right through it.

Batalha

The Gothic Mosteiro da Batalha (Monastery of the Battle) was, like Alcobaça, built in thanks for a military success. This time it

LOVE AND VENGEANCE

When he was heir to the throne, Pedro fell in love with Inês de Castro, lady-in-waiting to his wife Constanza of Castile. His father Afonso IV banished Inês, but when his wife died, Pedro sent for her. They lived together for ten years and she bore him four children. In 1355, on suspicion that Inês was working for Castile, some Portuguese nobles murdered her. Two years later, Afonso died and Pedro became king. Declaring that he had been secretly married to Inês, he had her body exhumed and seated on a throne, and forced the nobles to kiss her hand. The murderers were hunted down: two of them were caught and executed. Inês was reburied at Alcobaça, to be joined by Pedro when he died in 1367.

33

was not against the Moors, but the victory of the Portuguese under João I over the Castilians at Aljubarrota in 1385. Flying buttresses, pinnacles and lacy stonework adorn the exterior, and more than 100 statues surround the west door. Just inside is the imposing Founder's Chapel (Capela do Fundador) with the double tomb of João I and his queen, Philippa of Lancaster. Set in the wall are the smaller tombs of their sons, including Prince Henry the Navigator.

The arches of the Royal Cloister (Claustro Real) were decorated in the 16th century with a riot of Manueline stone-carving. But for the ultimate in that fantastic style, head outside and round to the east end of the church, where the Unfinished Chapels (Capelas Imperfeitas) stand open to the sky, just as they had been when they were abandoned by Manuel I in favour of a new location for the royal pantheon.

Fátima

Up in the hills east of Batalha, on May 13, 1917, three young shepherds saw a vision of "a lady all of light". According to one, Lucia dos Santos, the apparition instructed them to return on the 13th of every month until October, when she would bring messages. Word spread, and ever-increasing crowds came to the tiny village. On October 13, they saw blazing lights in the sky, and Lucia claimed that the lady, assumed to be the Virgin Mary, had spoken to her again, asking for a chapel to be built on the site and revealing three "secrets". The first was a call for repentance and peace; the second a prediction that Russia would spread terror and persecute the church. The third, divulged by John Paul II in May 2000, was interpreted as a prophecy of the attempt on his life in 1981.

The Catholic Church was initially reluctant to accept that miracles had occurred at Fátima, but believers flocked there in such great numbers that it eventually gained official approval and is now one of Christendom's most important places of pilgrimage. Millions come each year, with the biggest crowds on May 13 and October 13. A basilica in classical style faces a vast square, twice the size of St Peter's Square in Rome, and the village has become a sizeable town with hotels and many shops selling religious souvenirs.

Tomar

On a hillside above the charming little town of Tomar stands the most magnificent ensemble of medieval architecture in Portugal. Of the 12th-century Castle of the Templars (Castelo dos Templários), only the imposing walls remain. But within them are the buildings of the Convent of Christ, headquarters for the Order of the Knights Templar, and later for their successors the Order of Christ.

The oldest of these is the 16-sided, almost round Templars' oratory or Charola, which follows a favourite pattern of the knights. Inspired by the Holy Sepulchre at Jerusalem and other Byzantine chapels in the Levant, it has a high altar in the centre, surrounded by an octagonal screen of tall columns. In the early years of the order, its members are said to have attended mass on horseback, in a circle around the altar, but ready to ride off to battle at a moment's notice. The stone portal on the south side in the highly decorated plataresque style was added in the 16th century.

Cloisters and Chapterhouse

Adjoining the church on its west side is a two-storey extension added in about 1515, in the reign of Manuel. The lower level is an elegant chapterhouse, but to see its highlight you need to go outside, into the Renaissance Great Cloister, and up to the smaller Santa Bárbara Cloister. There, in the west wall of the chapterhouse, is the greatest triumph of Manueline stone-carving, a window so imaginative and complex that vis-

itors stand open-mouthed in wonder. All the nautical symbols so characteristic of the style are there: anchors, ropes, seaweed, billowing sails, and above them the cross of the Order of Christ.

The Town

Although overshadowed by the mighty castle walls and convent, the old town is worth exploring. Just south of its main square is Portugal's best-preserved medieval synagogue, now a Jewish museum (Museu Luso-Hebraico de Abraham Zacuto). On the river near the town is a huge waterwheel of Moorish design but much later construction. The church of Santa Maria houses the tomb of the 12th-century Templar Grand Master Gualdim Pais.

Coimbra

On a hill on the north bank of the Mondego River, Coimbra was an important Roman settlement then called Aeminium, and later occupied by the Visigoths and Moors. Christian forces under Ferdinand of Castile took it in 1064, and when Afonso Henriques declared the independence of Portugal in 1143, Coimbra became capital. Although Lisbon took over the role a century later, Coimbra remained the favourite of many later rulers. Its university is the oldest in the country—and was one of the first in the world. To 35 this day, Coimbra regards itself as a fountain of art and literature, with its own ancient customs, even its own brand of *fado*.

The University

The city long ago spread down to the river and across it, but the logical place to start a visit is where it began, at the top. Here, the Old University Quadrangle is lined on three sides by magnificent buildings from the 16th to 18th centuries. The open fourth side looks down over a view of the Mondego. The baroque Library (Biblioteca Joanina) built in about 1720 has a jewel-box interior of carved tropical woods and rich gilding.

Museu Machado de Castro

Housed in an old bishop's palace on the hilltop, with Moorish sections and Roman foundations, Coimbra's major museum has some fine medieval stone-carving and many other treasures. Most striking of all are the massive walls and arches, deep underground, which once were the street level and basements of the Roman city. They are the setting for a collection of Roman and Visigoth sculpture.

Sé Velha

The Old Cathedral, just below the University Quadrangle, was completed in the 12th century and built for defence as well as worship. It saw the coronations of several early kings, and perhaps the macabre enthronement of the exhumed body of Inês de Castro—there is some dispute about the site. The Gothic cloister is Portugal's oldest.

Baixa

In the Lower Town, down steep stone steps from the Old Cathedral, stands the elegant Arco de Almedina, a rebuilt Moorish arch. Running right past it, Rua Ferreira Borges is the main shopping street; to the south is the river, to the north the square called Praça 8 de Maio. The Church of Santa Cruz facing it dates from the early 16th century, the Manueline period, as seen in the cloisters. The tombs of Portugal's first two kings—Afonso I and Sancho I—were also rebuilt about that time.

South of the Mondego

Across the Santa Clara bridge from Coimbra and along the first road to the left is the restored convent church of Santa Clara-a-Velha. Pilgrims once flocked here to the tomb of the 14th-century Queen-Saint Isabel, known for her legendary generosity to the poor. But the site was so often flooded by the river that the convent on the hill above, Santa Clara-a-Nova, was built in the 17th century, with a new silver tomb. Along the river to the east, Fonte das Lágrimas (Well of Tears) is believed to be the site of the murder of Inês de Castro.

Conimbriga

A spur of high ground 15 km (9 miles) south of Coimbra and once an Iron Age Celtic stronghold, Conimbriga became an important Roman town, judging by the fine mosaics found when it was excavated. Many are on show in the modern museum next to the site. With the help of one of the booklets on sale there, a walk through the ruins shows how the fortunes of Conimbriga rose and then declined along with the power of the Roman Empire. Around AD 400, defence walls to hold off the barbarian invaders had to be built so hurriedly that many fine houses were sacrificed in the process. It was in vain; the town fell soon afterwards. The Visigoths later took over, but in the end even they abandoned the site and moved to Aeminium.

Figueira da Foz

The largest, liveliest resort on this coast has grown up around a sandy bay near the mouth of the Mondego.

Forta da Santa Catarina, where the Mondego meets the sea, was built in the 16th century to deter pirates. In 1808, students from Coimbra University seized it from the French invaders, thus enabling Wellington's British troops to land on the beach nearby, though many of the heavily laden soldiers were drowned when their boats capsized.

At the northern end of the sweeping curve of beach, the fishing village of Buarcos shelters behind its anti-pirate ramparts, no defence against today's tourists and developers who are turning it into a budget version of Figueira.

Aveiro

Seemingly stranded amid lakes and marshes—and nowadays by a network of modern highways—the old centre of Aveiro is cut through by canals, though it is hardly the "Venice of Portugal" that is sometimes claimed. As early as the 16th century its fishermen sailed to the Grand Banks of Newfoundland in pursuit of cod. But one night in 1575 a mighty storm threw up a sand bar that sealed off the estuary, cutting the port off from the sea. Only in 1808 was a channel dredged through the sandbars, opening the port to the ocean and bringing it back to life.

Excursion boats take visitors sightseeing and birdwatching on the Ria (lagoon), where a few traditional high-prowed *moliceiro* craft still harvest the seaweed for use as fertilizer on the sandy local soil.

37

OPORTO
Old City, Waterfront and Bolsa District,
Centre and West, Vila Nova de Gaia

Second in size to Lisbon, but first in every other way according to its inhabitants, the big city of the north gave its name not only to a drink but indirectly to Portugal itself. *O Porto* means simply "The Port". The Romans called their settlement near the mouth of the River Douro "Portus". Linked with Cale on the opposite bank it became Portucale, a name transferred to the young state formed when this area was conquered from the Moors.

The city began on the high ground north of the Douro where the river emerges from a steep-sided gorge. There's a dizzying view from the upper level of the 1886 Dom Luís I bridge, a huge cast-iron span soaring 60 m (200 ft) above the water which links the historic centre (Barredo) with Vila Nova de Gaia.

The Old City
Near the rocky summit, the granite 12th-century cathedral stands like the fortress it had to be in those days. The main feature of the cramped inte-

rior is a fine baroque silver altar, successfully hidden from invading French forces in 1809. João I and Philippa of Lancaster were married in the cathedral in 1387, cementing the alliance with England.

From the terrace in front of the cathedral, covering the steep slope down to the river, the old Barredo district is a medieval maze of narrow alleys and flights of steps, lined by tall, ramshackle buildings. Cut down through it to the waterfront if you want to expe-rience the atmosphere, but watch out for pickpockets and avoid the area after dark.

Waterfront and Bolsa District

Only a few small craft and excursion boats tie up along Cais de Ribeira nowadays, but people still come here to the markets or to eat in one of the little restaurants tucked into arches along the old city wall. Just uphill, the Casa do Infante, said to be the birthplace of Henry the Navigator, has been completely rebuilt and now houses the municipal archives and an exhibition centre. A block further from the river, the Feitoria

Inglesa is an 18th-century Georgian mansion built as headquarters and club of the British Port wine shippers association.

São Francisco

Next to the opulent Moorish-style Palácio da Bolsa (Stock Exchange), the 14th-century Gothic church of São Francisco has a stunning interior. Gilded carving added in the 18th century covers almost every surface, with an elaborate profusion of birds, twisting vines hung with grapes, angels and a giant Tree of Jesse,

PORT

The classic wine of Portugal was the result of a series of accidents. During England's frequent wars with France, and specifically in the 17th century when Britain banned the import of French wines, merchants turned to Portugal for supplies of red wine to replace claret from Bordeaux. Unfortunately the long, rough voyage across the Bay of Biscay often turned it to vinegar on the way. Then someone found that the addition of a shot of brandy stabilized it—as well as making it more potent. And if this addition was made early enough, it stopped the fermentation process while there was still some sugar unconverted into alcohol. The result was a sweet, strong wine, just what the English market demanded.

By the 18th century, Port was all the rage in Britain, helped by favourable import duties. Many British shippers established themselves in Oporto; some of their names are still familiar in the business today, such as Cockburn, Sandeman and Croft.

Vintage Port, the wine of a single excellent year, is the aristocrat of the Port world, although only a tiny fraction is in that category. A Vintage is declared only when the harvest and quality of the grape are considered to be exceptional (about one year out of three); the wine is bottled after 2–3 years in cask, and laid down for many years to mature. It forms a sediment (the "crust") and must be decanted before serving.

Late Bottled Vintage, also from a single year, spends about 6 years in cask before bottling. It doesn't need to be laid down or decanted.

Ruby Port is a blend of wines from different years, aged for a few years in cask. Red and fruity, it is ready for drinking. Tawny Port is similar, but made from lighter, more golden coloured wines.

White Port, made from white grapes and much less sweet than red or tawny, is served cold as an aperitif.

illustrating biblical stories. The church's museum has a fine collection of statuary and relics.

Centre and West

The main street leading north from the Dom Luís I bridge passes the São Bento railway station, worth a visit to see its enormous *azulejo* panels; one scene shows João I arriving for his wedding to Philippa.

Praça da Liberdade is a focal point of modern Oporto. Avenida dos Aliados is a garden boulevard running north, and immediately to the east are the city's most fashionable shopping streets.

On the northern edge of the old city, the 18th-century Torre dos Clérigos has become a symbol of Oporto. Over 200 steps lead to the top of the belltower and its unrivalled view.

Museu Soares dos Reis

Oporto's Museum of Fine Art, named after a noted 19th-century sculptor, is home of some of the best early Portuguese painting as well as collections of gold, silver, furniture and Oriental treasures reflecting Portugal's Age of Discovery and long history of trade with the Far East.

Vila Nova de Gaia

Directly across the Douro River from Oporto, ranged along the waterfront and up the hill behind

---

DOURO CRUISES

You can pass a restful hour or two on an excursion boat viewing Oporto from its best angle, the river. Or spend a week cruising up the river in luxury, passing through rocky gorges to the wine-growing regions, stopping to visit vineyards and *quintas*. Mooring at different ports of call each night, the voyage continues all the way to Barca de Alva at the Spanish frontier, the highest point on the Douro that large boats can reach. At various points along the way, passengers can take sightseeing tours to border castles and other historic sites.

---

are the *armazéms,* wine lodges. These cool stone warehouses are used to store Port wine after it is brought down from the vineyards. Sailing barges called *barcos rabelos* used to carry it downriver in barrels, but now it comes by road tanker; the surviving boats are just for show. Blending and bottling also take place here. Some lodges run tours and tastings, with the opportunity to buy.

High above the waterfront, the Pilar convent was Wellington's command post in 1809. He watched from these heights while his forces were stealthily ferried across the river in a few captured boats to expel the French.

▶ COSTA VERDE

Póvoa de Varzim, Barcelos, Viana do Castelo,
Valença do Minho, Monção, Ponte de Lima, Peneda-
Gerês National Park, Braga, Guimarães, Amarante

The green northwest is much more than a handful of ports and resorts. Inland is a region of small farms and even smaller fields, often hemmed in by vines growing up fences, a way of keeping the grapes cooler and the wines fresher. The valley of the River Lima is one of the prettiest in the country, and the River Minho, much of it marking the northern border with Spain, is lined with imposing fortresses. Braga and Guimarães vie with each other for the title of birthplace of the nation.

Póvoa de Varzim

An old fishing settlement 30 km (18 miles) north of Oporto has turned into one of the biggest resorts on this coast. A white wall of apartment buildings faces a huge stretch of sand, yachts fill the harbour and a casino offers live shows as well as gambling. Alongside all this fun and frolic, fisherfolk still mend their nets, and seaweed gatherers rake up the harvest of the tides for sale to farmers as a fertilizer.

Rates

Inland, 14 km (9 miles) east of Póvoa de Varzim is a village with one of the best Romanesque churches in Portugal. Built in the 12th century just after the Reconquest, it has three apses and a fine west door with original carved capitals.

Barcelos

A picturesque old town, Barcelos is famous throughout Portugal for two reasons. One is the enormous open-air market that fills the vast town square, Campo da Feira, every Thursday. The other is as the origin of the brightly painted cockerel which has practically become a national mascot.

There is more to see in Barcelos than the market. In the southwest corner of the Campo da Feira stands the domed octagonal Igreja do Senhor da Cruz, built around 1700, which set a fashion. Its white stucco walls and carved granite outlines were copied throughout Portugal, not only in churches but palaces too. The nearby Torre Nova, an old castle keep, houses the tourist information office and an excellent craft shop. Rua António Barroso leads

Bom Jesus do Monte in Braga: fervent pilgrims climb the stairs on their knees.

SAVED BY THE BIRD

The crowing cockerel has become a national emblem, but Barcelos is its true home. The story goes that a pilgrim passing through on his way to the shrine of Saint James in Santiago de Compostela was falsely accused of theft and sentenced to death. He made a last appeal to the judge who was just about to dine. Pointing to the roast bird on the table, he said: "May that cock crow if I am innocent." It duly rose from the plate and did so.

from here through the old town, where many fine houses survive from the 15th century.

The Palace of the Counts of Barcelos (Paço dos Condes), wrecked in the 1755 earthquake, is just a shell, but makes a good visit for the open-air archaeological museum of stone monuments from Roman times onwards. A 14th-century cross shows the saving of the hanged man in the legend of the cockerel.

Viana do Castelo

The port at the mouth of the River Lima knew great prosperity in the 16th century, when its merchants built the mansions that grace its old centre today. The fine town hall and Misericórdia Hospice facing the Praça da República

date from that time; the Gothic cathedral from a century earlier. Visitors flock to Viana in August for its famous folk and religious festivals, with great processions of floats, giant figures, elaborate costumes, dancing and drinking the wines of the surrounding Minho region. The beaches are south of the river, reached by an 1878 double-deck cast-iron bridge, one of the early projects of Gustave Eiffel.

Valença do Minho

Portugal's northern border with Spain has followed the wide River Minho since the 12th century, and successive kings built fortresses along it to guard the frontier. The best-preserved is Valença do Minho, where the old town is ringed by massive double walls in a star-shaped pattern, typical of the 17th century. They withstood several Spanish sieges, but nowadays the space between them is filled by market stalls selling to Spanish shoppers who cross the river to pick up bargains in clothing, drinks and shoes.

Monção

Another fortress town on the Minho, upriver from Valença, withstood numerous sieges during the long struggle to stay free from rule by Castile (and later by Spain). The tomb of Deu-la-Deu Martins in the Romanesque parish church recalls a local heroine who deceived a Castilian army in 1368. The Portuguese defenders were almost out of food, but she baked bread rolls with the last of the flour and tossed them over the wall to the besiegers, shouting that there was plenty more where they came from. Disheartened, the Castilians packed up and went home.

With no bridge, Monção sees little traffic from Spain; the old centre is charming. The region around produces good *vinho verde* wine, particularly from the Palácio de Brejoeira estate.

Ponte de Lima

The River Lima flows west from Spain through one of the greenest and most attractive valleys in Portugal. The bridge that gave Ponte de Lima its name was built by the Romans; its foundations and some of its arches were incorporated into a 14th-century reconstruction and Roman arches can still be seen near the right bank. The other end of the bridge,

now for pedestrians only, leads straight into the heart of the old town, one of the best architectural ensembles in the country. The tourist office in Praça da República has maps and recommendations for local walks.

The sandy river bank is the site of a market every second Monday. At other times it is used as a beach and a laundry.

Ponte de Barca

Upriver from Ponte de Lima, the present 15th-century bridge of ten arches took the place of the pontoon bridge which gave Ponte de Barca its name. The pleasant old town next to it is hemmed in by modern expansion, but the countryside around is unspoiled. A Tuesday market fills the promenade along the river bank with stalls selling local produce, clothing and household goods.

Bravães

Right next to the road, 6 km (4 miles) to the west of Ponte de Barca stands one of the most

TWO MIGHTY FORTRESSES The border with Spain is lined with castles built to deter invasion, and as cannons grew more powerful, they had to be made ever stronger. Representing the state of the art of defence in the 17th century, **Valença do Minho** in the north and **Elvas** on the eastern frontier are both encased in massive bastions.

important Romanesque churches in Portugal. The south and west doorways are surrounded by fine stone-carving depicting saints, birds, animals and mythological creatures. The interior has some wall paintings probably dating from the 16th century, discovered in the 1940s beneath layers of later paint.

Peneda-Gerês National Park

Northeast of Braga, the land rises as you approach the border with Spain. Artificial lakes formed by damming the fast-flowing rivers attract water-sports enthusiasts, while hikers head for the mountains and forests. The park headquarters are in the old spa town of Caldas do Gerês. Beyond it the road zigzags steeply upwards to Portela do Homem, the frontier post, where a cluster of tall Roman milestones shows that this was on an important imperial highway. The ancient road can still be traced, heading down through the woods near the Homem River, with many more milestones along the way

Braga

Not so long ago, Braga was wholly taken up with its role as religious capital. Priests and nuns were said to outnumber ordinary folk in the streets, and the archbishops of Braga frequently came off best in their many disputes with Portuguese kings. The church is not the power it once was, and industrial expansion has changed the balance of the population, but the Holy Week *(Semana Santa)* ceremonies here are still the most elaborate in the country.

The historic area lies to the west of the arcaded Praça da República; it is worth calling in at the tourist information office in a corner of the big square for a street plan. Just off the square is the 14th-century Torre de Menagem, the keep of a fortress which was once part of the city walls. From here, the pedestrian Rua do Souto passes the enormous Archbishop's Palace (Paço dos Arcebispos) and, almost opposite, the cathedral.

Sé

Mixing many styles from 12th-century Romanesque onwards, the cathedral has survived fires, wars, riots, and reconstruction which seems never ending. You have to take a tour to see the cloisters, fine choir gallery and the chapels round the north courtyard. One holds the tombs of Count Henry and his wife Teresa of Castile, parents of the first king, and the mummified body of the soldier-archbishop Lourenço Vicente who was wounded fighting the Castilians in 1385.

The interior of the Capela da Glória is covered with *mudéjar* frescoes in complex arabesque designs.

Bom Jesus do Monte

One of the most photographed sights in Portugal is the double stairway leading to the hilltop sanctuary church of Bom Jesus, 5 km (3 miles) east of Braga. The carved granite and white stucco baroque extravaganza was started in the 1720s. Ever since, pilgrims have climbed the hundreds of steps, sometimes on their knees, stopping at the numerous small shrines on the way. An unusual water-powered funicular was added in 1882; the car at the top of the hill has its tank filled and its extra weight then pulls the other car up. It's also possible to drive to the top.

Citânia de Briteiros

The back road from Braga to Guimarães which passes Bom Jesus do Monte also leads to the biggest pre-Roman archaeologi-cal site in Portugal. *Citânia* is the word for a Celtic fortified hilltop settlement, and Citânia de Britei-ros, 20 km (12 miles) southeast of Braga, is one of the few that didn't continue in use and be-come hidden beneath a modern town. Walls, narrow paved streets and the foundations of dwellings and other buildings cover the hill, but many of the most impressive monuments have been taken to the museum in Guimarães, named after the archaeologist, Martins Sarmento.

Guimarães

The birthplace of the first king of Portugal, Afonso Henriques, and later his first capital, can and does claim to be the "cradle of the nation". The historic centre is one of the most attractive and best-preserved in the country, and it has two superb museums. In short, Guimarães is one of the unmissable highlights of the north.

Most of the sights are inside the line of the old city wall. Some

THE THREE BEST MUSEUMS For the quality of its art and antiquities and the way they are displayed, the **Gulbenkian Museum** in Lisbon is supreme. The **Machado de Castro Museum** in Coimbra and the small but tastefully arranged **Alberto Sampaio Museum** in Guimarães use historic buildings to show off unique treasures.

47

parts of it survive, as well as the grim-looking castle, a keep and seven towers rebuilt many times since Afonso Henriques was born there in 1110 and which appears on Portugal's coat of arms.

The Ducal Palace (Paço dos Duques) just down the hill is mainly a modern creation, massively renovated in the 1930s on the orders of Dr Salazar to serve as a northern residence. The original 15th-century palace of the Dukes of Bragança was abandoned and fell into ruins after the third duke was executed for alleged treason. The present building houses fine antiques, tapestries and old weapons; it can be visited only on a guided tour.

In the town, two adjoining squares, Largo de Santiago and Largo da Oliveira, are lined with charming houses, palaces and former convents. The Colegiada da Nossa Senhora da Oliveira was enlarged by João I in thanks for the victory over the Castilians at Aljubarrota in 1385. A stone canopy of Gothic arches near the church marks a victory over the Moors. It stands on the traditional spot where the 7th-century Visigoth chief Wamba stuck his staff made of olive wood into the

A Gothic canopy marks the site of a 7th-century miracle.

ground, declaring that he would only become king if it sprouted leaves. Needless to say, it did so right away.

Museu de Alberto Sampaio

The cloisters of the convent building of Nossa Senhora da Oliveira now house the Alberto Sampaio Museum. One of its great treasures is the ragged tunic worn by João I at the Battle of Aljubarrota, another the silver triptych made to commemorate the victory. Downstairs, the 13th-century cloisters make a perfect setting for displays of *azulejos*, Gothic polychrome sculptures and medieval stone-carving.

Museu Martins Sarmento

West of the old centre, the archaeological museum founded by the man who excavated Citânia de Briteiros has one of the best collections of prehistory in the country, including massive stone-carvings. Housed in the rambling buildings, cloisters and court-yards of the former São Domingos convent, its displays are chaotic but intriguing. Most impressive are the carved lintels and doorways from Celt-Iberian sites, statues of Lusitanian warriors of the type who fought the Romans, and the mysterious seated granite figure called the Colossus of Pedralva, a figure 3 m (10 ft) tall used in fertility rites.

Santa Marinha da Costa

High up on a hillside 7 km (4 miles) southeast of Guimarães, the imposing 18th-century mon-astery would be worth seeing for its *azulejos* alone. Now that it has been converted into a *pousada,* you can stay in one of the monks' cells, turned into small but luxurious hotel rooms, and dine in palatial splendour.

Amarante

The setting beside the Tâmega River and the handsome old town centre make this one of the most attractive towns in the north. Next to a high, elegant bridge over the river, the Church of São Gonçalo stands on the site of an important Roman temple. The church was completed during the period of Spanish rule; among the statues in the upper gallery of its west front is one of Philip II of Spain.

The tomb of São Gonçalo inside the church dates from a much earlier period. It seems that Amarante was the focus of an ancient fertility cult, possibly pre-dating even the Romans, and this eventually became associated with the saint. São Gonçalo is the patron of spinsters seeking a husband. Over the centuries, hopeful hands have almost worn away the polychrome statue on his tomb. On his feast day, marriageable men and women give each other cakes in the form of phallic symbols. 49

Bragança, Chaves, Vila Real, Lamego, Viseu,
Guarda, Monsanto, Castelo Branco

The frontier region of the north-east, Trás-os-Montes ("beyond the mountains"), is as far from Lisbon as you can get in mainland Portugal. With a harsh climate, it was always poor, and people had to be forced or bribed to move there. In recent times large numbers have emigrated, but many have returned to set up businesses and build opulent new houses, in contrast to the traditional granite cottages. South and west of the mountains, Lamego and Viseu are centres of rich agricultural and wine-growing areas.

Bragança

The biggest of a chain of fortress towns intended to deter past Spanish threats is now a gateway for European trade, encouraged by improved road links. It was the stronghold of the dukes of Bragança, who were often rivals to the kings of Portugal until one of them succeeded to the throne himself in 1640.

Citadel and Castle

The hill above the modern town is ringed by granite walls and dominated by a castle keep now used as a military museum, worth a visit in its own right as well as for the view from the top. Be-neath it is a huddle of old houses, sadly dilapidated and threatened by a clearance plan. The Church of Santa Maria with its white tower has a fine painted ceiling, but the most intriguing building within the citadel is the five-sided Romanesque Domus, or council chamber, dating from the 12th century.

Chaves

The word means "keys", and this frontier town was certainly a key to northern Portugal. It was a Roman spa called Aquae Flaviæ (probably the actual source of the name Chaves) and its most remarkable sight is the Roman bridge of AD 104 carrying today's heavy traffic across the Tâmega River. On a hill above the bridge stands the 14th-century castle keep, surrounded by gardens and a collection of Roman and later stonework and sculptures.

Outeiro Machado

One of several prehistoric sites in the region stands 6 km (4 miles) west of Chaves. Signs pointing the way to *Arte Rupestre* direct you down a rough track through scrub, and eventually to a huge flattish rock that bears shallow carvings of axes, ladder shapes and other mysterious symbols. They are thought to date from around 700 BC, or perhaps earlier.

Vila Real

The regional capital has expanded fast, from an old centre high on a gorge where the Cabril and Corgo rivers meet. About 3 km (2 miles) east is a small country house, Solar de Mateus, made famous by millions of pictures seen on the round green bottles of a certain mass-production wine, Mateus Rosé. Its white stucco walls and extravagantly carved stonework detail are typical of the local version of baroque. Further out of town on the road to Sabrosa is Panóias, the site of an ancient sacrificial temple, probably Celtic but later taken over by the Romans.

Lamego

This prosperous wine town south of the River Douro has a fine museum with paintings by the 16th-century master Grão Vasco, and an interesting cathedral. But most visitors come to pray at the shrine of Nossa Senhora dos Remédios (Our Lady of Healing), at the top of a 686-step ceremonial double stairway built in 1771, on the lines of Bom Jesus do Monte near Braga. There's also a road to the top.

The fertile valley around Lamego produces both sweet and sparkling white wines, well-known throughout Portugal. Some of the producers offer tours and tastings.

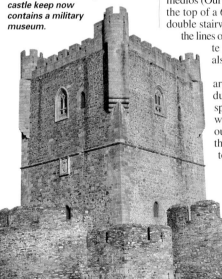

Bragança's forbidding castle keep now contains a military museum.

Viseu

An ancient hilltop town, Viseu may have been the stronghold of the Celt-Iberian hero Viriatus who held out against the Romans for years until his assassination in 139 BC. The granite hill was certainly a fortified Celtic settlement, and then a Roman base. The old part of Viseu still occupies the high ground, but in modern times the town has spread out below the hill. It's the gateway of the Dão wine-growing region to the east, along the valleys of the Dão and Mondego rivers.

The focus of the lower town is Praça da República (also known as Rossio), and good maps can be found in the tourist information office just off it in Avenida Gulbenkian.

Narrow streets lead up the hill to Praça da Sé (Cathedral Square) where the most striking building is not the plain cathedral but the white stucco and granite Misericórdia church which faces it. However, when it comes to interiors, the cathedral is far more rewarding, with fine stone vaulting and two-storey cloisters.

Museu de Grão Vasco

Viseu was the birthplace of the artist Vasco Fernandes, always called O Grão Vasco ("The Great Vasco"), who lived from about 1475 to 1541. His most famous works were painted for Viseu cathedral, notably the 14 scenes from the life of Christ for an altarpiece which are now displayed in the museum named after him. Rich colours, realistic details of dress and everyday life in 16th-century Portugal, together with striking portraiture, make a refreshing change from so much repetitive religious art.

Guarda

The highest city in Portugal, more than 1,040 m (3,400 ft) up on the northeastern slopes of the Serra da Estrela mountains, Guarda enjoys fresh, cool summers and endures bleak winters. Its name tells of its role as a stronghold against the Moors, and later the Spanish; even the granite cathedral looks like a fortress. It faces an impressive arcaded square, Largo de Camões, surveyed by a modern statue of Sancho I, the king who captured Guarda from the Moors in the 12th century.

Serra da Estrela Nature Reserve

Walkers, climbers, botanists and, in winter, skiers head for the scenic mountain range southwest of Guarda. The wool town of Covilhã at the southern end of the National Park makes a good base for exploring; its tourist office can supply maps and recommend guides. Caldas de Manteigas is an old-established spa and Linhares an ancient village whose parish church claims three paintings by Grão Vasco. Its castle is built on Roman foundations; Linhares was an important base during the pacification of the mountains.

Belmonte

Off the main road south of Guarda, Belmonte was another Roman settlement, now dominated by its restored castle. A curious three-storey tower on the northern edge of the town may have been the Roman *praetorium*, or military headquarters.

Belmonte was the birthplace of Pedro Alvarez Cabral, who "discovered" Brazil by chance on his way to the Cape of Good Hope in 1500. There's a model of his ship in the castle, and a statue of the Virgin Mary which he took on his voyage is kept in the parish church.

Monsanto

The houses of this ancient and altogether extraordinary village nestle among huge granite boulders, high up on the steep slopes of a pinnacle of rock. The road goes only part of the way up the hill; from there onwards you have to walk up steep alleys, steps and tracks to the fortified summit with its roofless Romanesque church and superb views of the surrounding plain.

Idanha-a-Velha

Down in the plain, not far from Monsanto, this quaint village was once an important Roman centre. You can still see the original paved street, passing through a twin-arched gateway in the town wall. The later Templars' Tower (Torre dos Templários) stands on the base of a Roman temple. Archaeologists are excavating the substantial remains of an early Christian basilica built by the Visigoths, also on Roman foundations. They have discovered a remarkable cruciform font, lined with marble, and some fine sculpture. The building was converted to a mosque by the Moors; the *mihrab* or niche facing Mecca can be seen in the eastern wall.

Castelo Branco

Now an attractive and expanding city of parks and flowers, Castelo Branco was fought over so often in the past that few ancient monuments remain. The castle of its name, built by the Templars in the early 13th century, lies in ruins. The most notable sights are the 18th-century baroque gardens of the former bishop's palace, with fountains and terraces, topiary and dozens of statues. Some of the figures represent signs of the zodiac, others depict all the kings of Portugal up to that date. The Spanish usurpers are included, but on a smaller scale! 53

THE ALENTEJO

Castelo de Vide, Marvão, Alter do Chão, Estremoz,
Vila Viçosa, Elvas, Évora, Monsaraz, Beja, Mértola

Meaning "beyond the Tagus", the Alentejo is the great plain that makes up most of south-central Portugal. The Romans turned it into a land of big farms, and huge tracts are still planted with wheat, interspersed with cork oaks. Summers are baking hot, and drivers heading south for the Algarve tend to view the Alentejo as an obstacle to be endured, but in early spring it can be fresh and green. A handful of towns—Évora, Estremoz, Beja—are well worth a visit for their historic monuments and atmosphere.

Castelo de Vide

The green hills of the Serra de São Mamede in the northeast corner of the Alentejo are quite unlike the rest. Castelo de Vide's springs made it a favourite with the Romans and Moors, and even today's local visitors bring bottles to take some of the famous water home.

Inside the walls of the pleasant old town are elegant squares, the little cobbled streets of the medieval Jewish quarter (Judiaria) with a 13th-century synagogue, and a hilltop citadel.

Marvão

A high ridge with near-vertical cliffs all round made the perfect defensive site, occupied from pre-historic times and further protected by powerful ramparts. A few years ago, emigration left the village almost deserted, but now the little white houses have been taken over by weekenders, artists and for tourist accommodation. The old church of Santa Maria houses an excellent museum, and the castle at the sharp end of the ridge offers dizzying views.

Alter do Chão

The town is one of the prettiest in the area, but the even bigger attraction for horse-lovers is the national stud farm, founded by João V in the mid-18th century. Dozens of magnificent Lusitanian thoroughbred horses graze the rolling pastures all around; spring is the time to see the enchanting foals. Visitors are welcome to tour the palatial buildings and museum.

Not far away, near Vila Formosa, stands the best-preserved Roman bridge in Portugal, if not the entire empire, with today's 50-ton trucks rumbling heedlessly across its sturdy arches.

The main street of the fortified village of Monsaraz seems to lead straight into the past.

Estremoz

Most buildings in the Alentejo are painted white to reflect the heat of the sun, but the citadel at Estremoz shines white for another reason: it is largely built of marble from the local quarries. It stands on a low hill, protected by multiple walls. Around it spreads the modern town, with a vast marketplace covered with stalls on Saturdays.

Inside the walls, the narrow, cobbled medieval streets lead to the main square, faced by the imposing Torre de Menagem (castle keep), the former royal palace, now converted into one of the most beautiful of the *pousada* hotels.

Vila Viçosa

When the dukes of Bragança left their grim northeastern stronghold, it was to move to Vila Viçosa. Even after the 8th duke became João IV in 1640, he and many of his successors liked to live in the ducal palace and spend their time in the happy hunting grounds of their nearby estates. The palace interior is dark and formal, with some rooms left as they were when Carlos I and his son Luis made their fateful journey to Lisbon in 1908, and their assassination.

Elvas

The border town on the main road from Madrid to Lisbon was turned into one of the most imposing fortresses in Europe in the 17th century. It was already well defended by medieval walls, but when Portugal regained its independence in 1640, it was further enclosed within star-shaped bastions of the type called Vaubanesque after the French military architect, the Marquis de Vauban, who perfected the design. They still stand, together with huge outworks which are almost as impressive.

CORK HARVEST

All over Portugal, but especially in the Alentejo, you'll see the bare and blackened trunks of cork trees, and sheets of the bark stacked beside the road or piled on the back of a truck. Doesn't it hurt the cork oak tree to have its bark removed every 10 years or so? Apparently not, though the poor thing looks as bereft as a newly shorn sheep. Portugal is the world's biggest producer of cork, much of it used for sealing wine bottles. The cost of cork and problems with variable quality have driven some wine makers to look for substitutes, but most fine wines stick to cork. A plastic cap just doesn't have the same cachet.

On the Lisbon side of Elvas, the towering multi-tiered Amoreira aqueduct soars over the valley, carrying water to the town. It looks like the Roman originals it imitates, but it was not completed until 1622.

Évora

The historic city at the heart of the Alentejo is also one of the most pleasant in Portugal, with an exquisitely preserved centre on the site of the Roman and Moorish town.

Whitewashed buildings lining its narrow cobbled streets include many palatial mansions dating from the 16th century when kings and queens preferred Évora to Lisbon. The old quarter then went through centuries of neglect; the population declined to less than a tenth of its peak. But that meant the houses were not modernized or replaced—hence their miraculous survival.

The university closed by the dictator Marquês de Pombal in the 18th century has reopened, and its thousands of students create a lively atmosphere.

Upper Town

Crowning the hill in the middle of Évora are the massive stone platform and 14 granite, marble-topped Corinthian columns of a Roman temple, the most notable relic of the period in Portugal.

Facing it, the Gothic and Manueline Convent of Lóios is now a hotel in the *pousada* network.

The municipal museum, to the south of the temple, occupies the former archbishops' palace. It has a fine collection of Roman sculpture, and striking paintings from the 15th and 16th centuries, with a remarkable altarpiece in 13 panels depicting the *Life of the Virgin* (c. 1500).

Directly downhill from the museum, the twin-towered granite cathedral dates from the 13th century. Its Gothic cloister shows Moorish influences. The cathedral's Sacred Art Museum includes reliquaries, vestments and various unusual religious relics.

The line of the Roman city wall, re-used by the Moors, can still be seen in the curve of the streets surrounding the hill.

Lower Town

To the west of the cathedral, Praça do Giraldo was once the Roman forum and is still the main square. Along Rua da República, the Church of São Francisco attracts curious visitors to its chapel, the Capela dos Ossos, which is completely lined with skulls and bones. They were dug up from cemeteries in the 16th century—there is a number of such macabre chapels in southern Portugal. A sign above the door says: "We, the bones which are 57

The Alentejo has been producing wines since Roman times, and they are getting better all the time.

here, are waiting for your bones". Across Praça 1 de Maio is a covered market full of local produce.

Monsaraz

East of Évora, close to the frontier with Spain, Monsaraz is a picturesque village packed inside the walls and bastions of a hilltop fortress. The little main street, lined with 16th and 17th-century whitewashed houses, leads to the castle, once a base of the Templar knights. Now its inner courtyard is used as a bullring.

Prehistoric monuments presumed to have been religious sites abound in the area. Just to the south of Monsaraz at Xerez is a square of standing stones with a taller one in the centre, 3.5 m (12 ft) high. And north of the village on the road to Outeiro is a still more prominent menhir, 5.5 m (18 ft) in height.

Beja

Visible from far away across the plain, the hilltop city founded by Julius Caesar is the highlight of the southern Alentejo. It stands today as it did then, at the centre of a wheat-growing region. Its high Torre de Menagem (castle keep) is a prominent landmark, with a superb view from the top, and several sections of the ancient city wall are still visible.

Museu Regional

Beja's main museum has some interesting exhibits, but the real star of the show is the building that houses them—the former Convento de Nossa Senhora da Conceição. The 15th-century baroque chapel is full of carving, gilding and multi-coloured marble; the cloisters are lined with precious old *azulejos*. Most exuberant of all is the tiled and painted chapterhouse. The grid of pierced clay tiles in the Coat of Arms room is said to be the one through which the nun Mariana Alcoforado first saw her French lover, Count Chamilly, who was fighting against the Spanish. The volume of five letters she is supposed to have written to him, published in 1669 as *Love Letters of a Portuguese Nun*, is a classic of Portuguese literature.

Igreja de Santo Amaro

On one side of the castle, a church originally built by the Visigoths on Roman foundations is now the most important museum of Visigothic stone-carving in the country. Little has survived from that era, the 6th and 7th centuries, and this well-displayed collection is a rare chance to see some of the best examples.

Mértola

The road from the southern Alentejo to the eastern end of the Algarve passes close to the walls of a fascinating old fortress town. Mértola was built at the confluence of the Guadiana and Oeiras rivers, with its 13th-century castle on the high ridge between them. In the old quarter below its walls are buildings imaginatively adapted as museums of Roman and Islamic art and artefacts. Most remarkable of all is the Igreja Matriz (parish church) near the castle gate. Almost alone in Portugal, it retains the layout and appearance of the 11th-century mosque that it once was, a single hall divided into aisles by twelve columns, and a *mihrab*, the niche indicating the direction of Mecca.

4

THE FOUR FINEST CHURCHES Among countless interesting examples from every era, a few stand out: the almost circular Templars' church at **Tomar**; the Cistercian abbey church of **Alcobaça** with the amazing tombs of Pedro and Inês de Castro; the 14th-century Gothic masterpiece of **Batalha**; and at **Mértola** the parish church which looks like a mosque.

Sagres, Lagos, Portimão, Silves, Albufeira, Fóia, Faro,
Loulé, Olhão, Tavira, Vila Real de Santo António

Mountains cut the southernmost region of Portugal off from the rest until rail and road links were built in modern times. It was an independent province under the Moors, who stayed more than 500 years. Even after the Reconquest, Portugal's rulers took the title "King of Portugal and the Algarve", emphasizing its separateness. From small beginnings in the 1950s, it has become one of Europe's premier holiday destinations.

From Cape St Vincent in the west to the Spanish border in the east, the Algarve looks south over 160 km (100 miles) of Atlantic coastline. The beaches of the eastern part, called the Sotavento (leeward) coast, are flat and expansive—and so wide that it can be a long trek to the water. The western section, called the Barlavento (windward) coast, has eerie rock formations, cliffs and caves. And the further west you go, the smaller and more secluded the beaches become.

Inland are orchards of citrus fruit, olives and almonds and the uplands beyond are covered with pines, eucalyptus and wild flowers. Artisans keep alive the old skills, although most of the buyers these days are tourists.

Sagres

The little port near the western end of the Algarve has been growing rapidly since a new road made it easier to reach. The beaches are small and rather exposed, and the water can be cold, but Sagres attracts scuba divers, bird-watchers and those who just like to go to the end of things.

Ponta de Sagres

To the west of the town, a promontory 60 m (200 ft) above the waves is where, tradition says, Henry the Navigator established his School of Navigation. Blame Sir Francis Drake for the lack of certainty; not much was left after his raid in 1587, and still less after the earthquake of 1755. The fortress that dominated the site was rebuilt then, and has been heavily restored in recent years, with a coat of cement that gives it the look of a stage set. Inside, a small white chapel dates from the 18th century, but other buildings are more recent.

Below the main gate is a vast mariner's wind compass (*Rosa dos Ventos*) marked in stone on the ground, but strangely there's no record as to when it was installed. Most scholars suggest the early 19th century, though it may

PATRON SAINT

Cabo de São Vicente got its name from the 4th-century martyr-priest, St Vincent. During the Islamic occupation, his body was hidden in the Algarve, but as the centuries went by no-one could remember where. After the Christian Reconquest, the legend goes, searchers failed to find the saint's remains—until a pair of ravens led them to the spot. Then, as the relics were being shipped to Lisbon, the loyal ravens flew along. St Vincent is Lisbon's patron saint; the seal of the city shows the ravens and a sailing ship.

have replaced an older, worn-out version. So most of the history here is in the imagination, but the prince's achievements in sending mariners beyond sight of land are as real as today's satellite-guided ships turning this busy corner of the Atlantic.

Cape St Vincent

Here at the southwestern tip of Europe, the stunted bushes have been bent by Atlantic gales, and the low-slung houses are dug in for self-defence. Yet on a cloudless day when the ocean is as calm as a pond, the "end of the world" seems more like the beginning. The families of the lighthouse guardians huddle together in a compound, once a monastery, at the base of a red-topped beacon. You can look straight down the cliffs to the ocean and roam around the lighthouse complex, where the keepers' wives take the sun, crocheting baby shoes and bedspreads.

Aljezur

The ruins of a castle—all that was left after the 1755 earthquake—stand on a hilltop, the highest of three in this curiously arranged town on the Algarve's west coast. There are two churches; the newer one up the hill was built by a bishop who tried to move the town to a higher altitude to get away from the pesky mosquitoes, but most of the townsfolk failed to follow.

Aljezur is the gateway to some of the wide-open beaches of the west coast, notably Praia de Monte Clérigo and Praia de Arrifana.

Lagos

Phoenicians, Romans and Moors developed Lagos, and parts of the ancient city wall, much restored, still stand guard. But a modern statue of Henry the Navigator, holding a sextant and gazing out at the harbour, recalls the port's most memorable role in history. Henry was Governor of the Algarve, and this was his capital. His caravels, designed and built in Lagos, sailed from here into

Praia da Luz is one of the best beaches near Lagos.

the unknown. Captives brought back from Africa were put up for auction in a small arcade, marked "Mercado de Escravos" (slave market), on the northeast side of what is now Henry the Navigator Square.

Igreja de Santo António

The interior of St Anthony's Church all but explodes with 18th-century rococo art. On the gilt walls and altar, a convention of angels hold up columns and each other. This was the church of the Lagos regiment of the Portuguese army, and a gravestone in the floor commemorates its Irish commander, Col. Hugh Beatty.

Museu Regional

Next to the church, the museum has displays of archaeology, crafts and ethnography including African sculptures caricaturing Portuguese colonial officials. The religious art includes 16th-century vestments worn at a mass said for King Sebastião just before his suicidal crusade to North Africa. A startling modern statue of Sebastião by João Cutileiro, in Praça Gil Eanes, pictures him as a weird astronaut with a mop of hair covering a cartoon face.

Beaches

Lagos is not a resort in itself, but nearby Praia da Luz, once a whaling station, exploits its big, curving bay for water sports. Burgau and Salema to the west are fishing villages now in the grip of tourism. East of Lagos are Meia Praia and Alvor, long sandy beaches favoured by windsurfers. In the old town of Alvor, the parish church has a carved portico in the Manueline style.

Ponta da Piedade

Between Lagos and Luz, the wind and waves have sculpted evocative rock formations, both free-standing and attached to the cliffs. The scene is impressive from above, and even more so from the sea aboard one of the excursion boats.

Portimão

Portus Magnus to the ancient Romans, the town at the mouth of the Arade River became Portimão, a vital fishing port, and in recent years an important commercial centre. Tourists from the nearby resorts are attracted by some of the Algarve's best shops, many of them in pleasant pedestrians-only streets.

A few years ago the fishing fleet was exiled from the middle of town to a new harbour across the river. The old quay now specializes in pleasure craft and excursions. On the quayside, delicious giant sardines are cooked on charcoal grills.

Praia da Rocha

The beach that launched a million postcards, Praia da Rocha is within walking distance of Portimão. Dotted with splendid free-standing rock formations, the spacious beach can't be disturbed, but the cliffs behind it are heavily burdened with high-rise apartments, spreading ever further inland.

High above the eastern end of the beach and the mouth of the Arade River, the fortress of Santa Catarina looks like a convincing bastion. But just walk through the gates and you will find that the interior has been converted into an open-air restaurant. Take a stroll round the walls for the views along the coast.

Carvoeiro

Holiday villas rise like an amphitheatre behind the small beach of Carvoeiro, hemmed in by cliffs. Yet somehow the fishing boats pulled up on the sand make it seem as if nothing has changed since simpler days. The coast along here is riddled with caves and coves; snorkellers have a field day.

Armação de Pêra

The former fishing village of Armação de Pêra has been overtaken by high-rise tourism, but the golden beach is still a winner. Nearby, on a promontory between two beaches stands a simple chapel dedicated to Our Lady of the Rock (Nossa Senhora da Rocha), where for centuries sailors and fishermen prayed before going to sea.

Silves

Inland from Portimão, rising above a lazy river among citrus orchards and weeping willows, Silves, then called Xelb, was for five centuries the Moorish capital of the Algarve. Its gardens, palaces and culture were famous throughout the Islamic world. All that came to an end in 1189. In an echo of the fall of Lisbon 42 years before, Sancho I recruited some Crusaders to help besiege and take the city. As at Lisbon, the defenders surrendered and an orderly hand-over was agreed, but the Crusaders indulged in an orgy of pillage and slaughter. Although the Moors recaptured it two years later and held it until their final departure from the Algarve in 1249, Silves never recovered. The river which had been a highway of commerce gradually silted up in the 15th century. Now anything bigger than a rowing boat is liable to run aground.

The Castle

Much fought over and much restored, the old red citadel surmounting the town is a solid reminder of a vanished era of great-

HOMESICKNESS REMEDY

This Arabian Nights story is supposed to have happened in many places, from Persia to Turkey to Spain. But the Algarve claims the legend as its own. Once upon a time, an Arab potentate took a Nordic princess as his wife. She pined for the snows of home, and fell into a decline. Distraught, the king ordered all the fields surrounding his castle to be planted with almond trees. As spring arrived, the sight of a sea of white almond blossom revived her. To this day the annual spectacle lifts the spirits.

ness. The Great Tower faces north, for that was the route attackers customarily chose. You can wander along the perimeter walls and imagine the battles and sieges while looking out onto the town, river and farms. Inside the battlements all is peaceful, except during the summer beer festival.

Santa Maria da Sé

Founded in the 13th century, the cathedral hasn't had a bishop in residence since 1579 when the town was eclipsed by Faro. Then came the 1755 earthquake, on top of earlier quake damage. Gothic in the beginning but tending to the baroque over centuries of repairs and alterations, the cathe- 65 dral somehow retains its early dignity, and the high vaulted interior is impressive.

Museu de Arqueologia

In 1990 a new Municipal Museum of Archaeology was opened in a very old mansion in Rua das Portas de Loulé, near an archway which was once a barbican gate. The exhibits, ranging from Stone Age axe-heads to 15th-century pottery, are well chosen and displayed. Some ceramics from the Moorish era are more beautiful than almost any available today. An Arab well with spiral steps descending to a depth of 15 m (50 ft) was found in the house and is now on view.

Fóia

The summit of the Algarve, at just over 900 m (nearly 3,000 ft), Fóia is a cool escape from summer's heat at the beach. Actually, it's often so windy that you may decide to buy a sweater, sold on the spot by the merchants who meet the excursion coaches. On a clear day the view can reach from the Sagres peninsula to the beaches of Portimão.

Monchique

In the hilly market town of Monchique, the whitewashed parish church is distinguished by a Manueline portal decorated with carved knots. Above the town are the ruins of a 17th-century Franciscan monastery, abandoned after the great earthquake. The hills of the Serra de Monchique, which protect the Algarve from northern winds, get enough rainfall to encourage the most varied vegetation—eucalyptus, arbutus, pine, oak, and roadside flowers.

Caldas de Monchique

A spa first developed by the Romans, this leafy backwater south of Monchique has lost most of its glamour nowadays, but you can still sample the health-giving if smelly water as it emerges piping hot from the source. It is bottled, and served cold in bars and restaurants all over the province.

Albufeira

The Algarve's biggest resort somehow keeps its sense of balance. The beaches may be swarming with sunbathers, but fishermen still go about their business; a little crowd greets every arriving boat to look over the catch. The cobbled streets of the old town are devoted to commerce, as they must have been in Moorish times; the outdoor market deals in everything from pets to live chickens for the cooking pot. Albufeira's natural defensive position kept the Moors entrenched after most of the Algarve had fallen to the Christian Reconquest.

Old Town

The old centre is barred to traffic —only pedestrians can tread the mosaic tiles. Restaurants and bars keep the area lively, and multilingual touts at their doors try to drag in the customers, but it's all quite relaxed. The hills above the town are built over with hotels; a tunnel cuts through the cliff to the beach, framed by surreal rocks, and to the neighbouring fishermen's beach.

Olhos de Água

A fine sandy beach has attracted development, construction and traffic jams to a once-quiet stretch of coast. A natural phenomenon here is an undersea freshwater spring, visible and usable only at low tide. When the tide comes in, the pressure of the submerged spring is said to create tricky tidal patterns. Olhos de Água means "eyes of water", and the fishermen paint all-seeing eyes on the prows of their boats, as seamen have done for centuries to ward off danger.

Vilamoura

The high-rise apartment blocks and hotels of the Vilamoura holiday complex face the Algarve's biggest marina, haven for hundreds of yachts from the seven seas. Water sports, golf courses, tennis, horse riding, fitness centres, restaurants of many kinds, and nightlife—they're all in the master plan, plus a surrounding arc of villa colonies.

The promoters of Vilamoura weren't the first to see the virtues of the site. The ancient Romans built a harbour nearby and developed a fish-salting industry. The Cêrro da Vila excavations show the Roman water system, walls and mosaics.

Quarteira

While Vilamoura is a custom-made resort, the next town eastward is a real fishing village that has been overwhelmed by high-rise hotels and blocks of flats next to its golden sand beach. Still, the traditional weekly outdoor market is a treat for the tourists, as well as an essential for the locals.

Vast Resorts

Vale do Lobo is a planned resort community with a hotel, beach, villas and first-class golf and tennis facilities. The name means "valley of the wolf", but the only howls come from golfers who miss a putt.

Just to the east, Quinta do Lago is an even more luxurious affair, also with a hotel, golf courses and tasteful villas widely dispersed in a landscaped park, next to a beach and nature reserve. Resorts like these are so big that a car is essential for getting from the villa to the beach or shops.

Faro

The capital of the Algarve can feel more like a provincial backwater than a dynamic centre of tourism and commerce. Enhancing the impression is the sight of the low-rise old town with its whitewashed houses and palm trees, and the sleepy, shallow pleasure port on its doorstep. The Moors arrived from North Africa in 714 and made Faro the capital of a principality, until Portugal's King Afonso III reconquered it in 1249.

The Port

Since the tidal flat silted up, only small boats can manoeuvre under the low railway bridge that provides the sole access; you can watch them coming and going from the waterfront promenade. Just inland, the Jardim Manuel Bivar is a palm-shaded municipal garden with flowering trees, children's swings and slides, handicrafts stalls and a popular café.

Walled Town

The way into the old walled town is through the Arco da Vila, a fine 18th-century arch with a stork's nest atop the bell tower. (The tourist office is just next door.) Worn cobbled streets lead to the cathedral, on a site said to have been used first for a Roman temple, then a Visigothic church, then a mosque. Finally the Ro-manesque-Gothic church was built in the middle of the 13th century, and expanded and repaired after earthquakes and other disasters. Inside, a brilliantly decorated baroque organ is a highspot, with trumpet-blowing angels and other joyous images.

Archaeological and Ethnographical museums

The Museu Arqueológico occupies an old, whitewashed convent virtually next door to the cathedral. Among prehistoric and Roman artefacts dug up in Faro and its suburbs is a magnificent 2,000-year-old Roman mosaic portrait of a bearded Neptune.

In the town centre, just beyond the pedestrians-only shopping zone, the Museu Etnográfico Regional tells the story of Algarve culture through typically furnished houses, crafts and traditional costumes.

Igreja do Carmo

Opposite Faro's main post office is the 19th-century Carmelite church, its graceful towers and façade hemmed in by the modern city. The interior has some notable baroque wood-carvings and paintings, while the somewhat macabre Capela dos Ossos

Off to work in Faro, the low-key provincial capital.

(bone chapel), reached through a side entrance, was constructed from the skulls and bones of monks and parishioners.

Faro's Beaches

Sand bars protecting Faro from the open sea give the city its beaches. Out past the airport, Ilha de Faro is linked to the mainland by a bridge, so it tends to attract crowds of locals and tourists. If the waves on the ocean side are too strong, move to the lagoon side, where the water is usually calm. The sandy shores of neighbouring Ilha da Barreta are only accessible by boat.

Igreja de São Lourenço

A few miles west of Faro, a white country church on a hill overlooking the busy highway contains a wonderful surprise. One of the few Algarve churches spared by the 1755 earthquake, it was built early in the 18th century after the villagers' prayers to St Lawrence were answered: desperate for water, they suddenly discovered a gushing spring. The inner walls and vaulted ceiling are all but covered in *azulejos*, blue-and-white glazed tiles recounting the life of the saint.

Estói

Inland from Faro, this village has an 18th-century palace (Palácio do Visconde de Estoi) with faded charm, built on a brilliantly landscaped hill site above a goldfish pool and garden. The palace is awaiting renovation, but the exterior and garden are elaborately decorated with *azulejos* of plump nudes and solemn portraits.

Milreu

The Roman ruins within walking distance of Estói have yielded statues, pottery, jewels and mosaics, now kept in museums in Faro, Lagos and Lisbon. Probably the country villa of a Roman aristocrat, the site has a well-preserved sunken bath with mosaics of fish, and the ruins of a Visigothic basilica which had originally been a pagan temple dedicated to water gods.

Alte

The hill village of Alte was once proclaimed the Algarve's most picturesque; its parish church has a Manueline portal and there are plenty of pretty, whitewashed houses with architectural and decorative flourishes. Outside the village, a stream burbles through a tree-shaded park on its way to irrigate the citrus, fig and pomegranate trees in the valley below.

Loulé

A dynamic regional centre, with a modern shopping zone, Loulé still keeps to its small-town pace. The great attraction in this inland

LOULÉ • OLHÃO ◄

market town is the market itself, a Moorish-style building with big displays of produce and handicrafts. Nearby are the remains of a castle, converted into a museum, and of the city wall, built during the Moorish occupation. The battlements slice through the centre of town, so you can climb one of the towers and look down on the crowded maze of streets, another reminder of Arab times.

Loulé's festivals are the most colourful of the Algarve. At Carnival time, flower-decked floats roll through the streets and participants affect far-out costumes. On Easter Sunday a mostly solemn procession carries an image of Nossa Senhora da Piedade, the town's patron saint, down from a 16th-century hilltop shrine.

Olhão

They call it the "cubist city", because of the old town's boxy whitewashed houses with flat terraces instead of the red-tile roofs typical of the Algarve. Many of the houses have outside stairways leading to lookout towers, ideal for checking up on fishermen husbands or possible pirate attack. The architectural style, and the town itself, developed long after the Moors left, but the inspiration was North African, brought here by Olhão boatmen who traded with Morocco in the 18th and 19th centuries.

In 1808, volunteers with primitive weapons killed or captured the French garrison and proclaimed the restoration of independence. When the Portuguese king João VI, exiled in Brazil, received the news—hand-carried across the Atlantic by daring local sailors—that Napoleon's troops had been routed from the country, he bestowed the title, "Noble Town of Olhão of the Restoration".

Fishermen from Olhão sail to the Arctic and southern oceans in search of cod, hake and halibut. Closer to home, they drag in tons of sardines, most of which are

FIVE COLOURFUL FESTIVALS Almost every town has its saint's day, with processions, dances, perhaps fireworks or bullfights; **Lisbon** honours St Anthony and **Oporto** St John, both in June. **Loulé** puts on the Algarve's biggest Carnival parade; **Viana do Castelo** holds a huge religious and folklore festival in August; **Braga** stages the greatest celebrations in Holy Week.

A former tuna-fishing town, Tavira is now awash in charm and tranquillity.

gobbled up by the local canning factory. The fish market is well worth a look, and next door, in an identical hangar-like building on the waterfront, is the everything-else market, with inviting displays of fruits, vegetables, meat and even hardware.

Offshore Islands

The low-lying islands that protect Olhão's harbour are easily reached by ferries. Ilha de Armona is only 15–20 minutes away, with miles of beaches; Ilha da Culatra, more distant, mixes fishing villages and holiday beach huts. The barrier islands form the seaward boundary of the Ria For-

mosa nature reserve, extending from west of Faro nearly to the Spanish border.

Tavira

Fishermen and aristocrats have always coexisted in this small city of great charm, distinguished churches and discreet mansions. The Romans first built the seven-arch stone bridge spanning the River Gilão in the middle of town—much restored but still essentially the original design (pedestrians only). Down at the quay, fishermen repair their nets and tourists take the ferry to Ilha de Tavira, a giant sandbank. Many of the city's churches suffered in the earthquake of 1755, and so did the castle, of which only the walls remain. Santa Maria do Castelo, the castle's church, dates from the 13th century, when it was built on the ruins of a mosque. Here João I knighted his sons, including the future Henry the Navigator, after their conquest of Ceuta on the coast of northern Africa.

Monte Gordo

The Algarve ends with a whale of a beach—and a jumble of hotels, apartments and a casino. Where they peter out, there are pine trees, dunes and plenty of room to escape the crowds.

Vila Real de Santo António

Now a busy fishing port, this odd-looking city rose from nothing in five months of 1774 in a bid to impress the Spaniards across the Guadiana River. The idea came from the Marquês de Pombal, who rebuilt Lisbon after the earthquake; Vila Real follows the same grid plan as the capital's Baixa district. The main square features black and white cobblestones in a sun-ray pattern emanating from an obelisk dedicated to Pombal's patron, the king.

Local merchants energetically push whatever appeals to visitors from across the river. Now that a modern bridge links the two

CHIMNEYS

Since Moorish times the Algarve skyline has been beautified by delicately filigreed chimneys. House-proud Algarvians commission latticed chimneys even if they don't have a fireplace. Generally white, they come in many fanciful forms, like mini-minarets or mushrooms. In olden days they were carved from tree trunks, but ceramic or cement is the modern medium.

countries just north of Vila Real, the ferry service is secondary. Either way, it's an easy trip to the Andalusian town of Ayamonte.

Castro Marim

In Roman times the Guadiana River marked the dividing line between the provinces of Lusitania and Baetica, the forerunners of Portugal and southern Spain. The Romans left a hilltop fortress, adapted by the Moors during five centuries of occupation. After the Reconquest Castro Marim was the headquarters of the Order of Christ (successors of the Knights Templar) until they moved to Tomar. In the 17th century, when relations with Spain had deteriorated, the Portuguese built a second fort dominating the river. The marshland below the fortifications is now a nature reserve, Reserva Natural do Sapal. 73

Cultural Notes

Azulejos

Painted and glazed ceramic tiles are the quintessential Portuguese decorative art, found everywhere from old churches and palaces to your hotel bathroom. The technique came from North Africa during the Moorish occupation, when artists were restricted by the rules of Islam to calligraphic and abstract designs, in blue, green, yellow and white. After the Reconquest, Portuguese artists were free to show the human form; they illustrated historical events, biblical stories, saints' lives, and even used the tiles as vehicles for satire and to make political points. Around 1660, the fashion changed. Multicoloured designs were out; everything had to be in blue and white, perhaps under the influence of Dutch Delft. Blue and white is still the most popular colour scheme.

Azulejos were widely used to put an impressive—and waterproof—façade on houses. Some of the best displays are found in cafés, where they make an easy-to-clean surface as well as a striking decor. Old and rare *azulejos* are collectors' items nowadays; startling sums are asked for early examples, but dealers will also attempt to charge grossly inflated prices for very ordinary tiles.

Camões

In the age of Cervantes and Shakespeare, Portugal's national poet, Luís Vaz de Camões, set his nation's literary standards for the centuries. His most dazzling work, the epic poem *Os Lusíadas*, links Greek mythology with the exploits of the Portuguese explorers.

Born in about 1524 to an impoverished but aristocratic family, Camões seems to have enjoyed a riotous, spendthrift youth. Frequently in conflict with authority, he was banished in 1547 to the little town of Constância, near Tomar, for having the temerity to write a love poem to a lady who had also caught the eye of João III. By 1553 he was back in Lisbon and in trouble again for street brawls.

Then followed 17 years of travel to the faraway places of the Portuguese empire. Perhaps exiled again, or maybe seeking his fortune, he served in Ceuta, Goa and Macau, and was shipwrecked on the coast of Indochina. He was destitute in Mozambique when a sympathetic friend paid for his passage home in 1570. His great epic was published two years later, but in the long years of his absence such work had gone out of fashion, and his genius was only recognized after his death.

Nowadays, his lyric poems are as highly regarded as *Os Lusíadas*. He was given a small state pension but continued to spend beyond his means and died on the verge of poverty in 1580.

Fado

The intensely emotional songs known as *fado* may derive from the lamentations of African slaves, but whatever their origins, they are now the most Portuguese of music forms. A short performance is often included in a show staged for tourists, but for something more authentic, it's necessary to find a *Casa de Fado* catering for a local audience. Dinner is usually served first, and the show doesn't start until late. At last the lights dim, the audience goes quiet and two guitarists begin the accompaniment. A spotlight picks out the singer, dressed in black, as she starts to wail her song of loss, yearning, regret and nostalgia. All these and more are conveyed by the Portuguese word *saudade*, a psychological condition leading to sentimental fatalism. It may be difficult for foreigners to fathom, but that's what gives *fado* such power.

Manueline architecture

Reigning from 1495 to 1521, Manuel I presided over the golden age of Portuguese discoveries. And spanning roughly the same period, a new style of architecture evolved in Portugal. Developed from late-Gothic, it first added details with nautical themes, with stone-carving of rope, sails, anchors and sea creatures. Then came more elaborate celebrations of the wonders of exploration: carved globes, exotic plants, fruits and coral embellishing church doors, columns and capitals.

Soon the vogue swept all before it: ancient churches were given new doorways; the mansions of the rich had Manueline flourishes (though people wouldn't have recognized the word, a 19th-century coinage). Vast projects were begun in which the organic designs covered practically the whole surface of a building, with a density of carving to rival the great Hindu temples. No coincidence—Vasco da Gama had reached India and brought back drawings of such marvels. Then, almost as quickly as it had appeared, Manueline went out of fashion. The Unfinished Chapels at Batalha were left roofless and Portugal rejoined the mainstream, building to the rules of the Renaissance.

Only one building was completed in the Manueline style, the perfect little Torre de Belém on the Tagus below Lisbon. Nearby are the elaborate south door and cloisters of the Jerónimos monastery, but the epitome of Manueline must surely be the west front of the Chapterhouse at Tomar.

75

Shopping

Copper and brass, pottery and ceramic tiles, basketry and leatherwork, embroidery and lace are still produced in quantity for the home market as well as for the visitors. Look in city craft shops, roadside outlets and the weekly markets held in most towns. Or you may come upon artisans at work in the villages. Buying from the source is not a guarantee of a bargain, but you'll have the memories to go with the souvenir.

Where?

Only Lisbon and Oporto have a wide choice of shopping: elegant department stores, fashion boutiques, modern malls such as the capital's Colombo Centre, and small traditional shops as well. In the Algarve, Portimão, Faro and Loulé offer the best selection, and almost every little town has its mini-supermarket stocking the essentials. The resorts have stores that can supply most holiday needs. For fun and variety, don't miss the regular open-air markets, giant gatherings such as those at Barcelos (every Thursday) and São Pedro de Sintra (every second Sunday) or more modest local events.

What?

Portugal used to be renowned for its low-priced clothing, shoes and other everyday goods. Although fast catching up with the rest of the European Union, there are still savings to be made: witness the coachloads of Spanish shoppers in the border towns, staggering home with goods by the sackful, from woollens and children's clothes to bottles of port.

Traditional Crafts

Brass and copperware have been a speciality since Moorish times. Craftsmen can be seen at work in Loulé in the Algarve, hammering away at trays, candlesticks, decorative jugs and humbler pots and pans. Perhaps you have enjoyed eating *amêijoas na cataplana*, steamed clams in a metal dish like a wok with a hinged lid. If so, whether you use it for decorating your kitchen or actually cooking in it, a *cataplana* is one of the most typical items you can buy.

More for the kitchen: ceramic bowls, plates, pitchers and cups, hand-painted in bright colours to remind you of summer sunshine. Portugal also produces tons of rough pottery, such as garden planters and amphorae, and the pots that local fishermen use as octopus traps. You can take home a miniature of an Algarve chimney no bigger than a pepper-shaker or perhaps brighten up your kitchen or patio with *azulejos*—a single painted tile or a whole illustrated ensemble. Given time, the makers will produce a wall panel to your own specifications.

In some fishing ports, once the nets are mended the women traditionally turn to more delicate needlework: embroidery or lace. You'll often see them working in the doorway of their home, or more congenially in groups in some shaded corner. In the shops you'll find everything from bedspreads to table napkins. The best, from the island of Madeira, are also sold all over mainland Portugal.

Bobbin lace is still made in the northern town of Vila do Conde. And from Arraiolos in the Alentejo come beautiful, though expensive, handmade rugs in striking designs and colours.

Knitwear may be a practical purchase if you have nothing for a cooler evening. The rugged, handmade pullovers of the sort that fishermen wear come from the hill country where the sheep are sheared, and the wool is washed, combed and spun. Cleverly, they're often sold where it's windy—at Sagres and Fóia.

Gold and silver filigree, another Moorish legacy, turns up in earrings and brooches intricately fashioned in the form of model caravels or in abstract modern designs.

Wickerwork comes in many varieties—mats, hats, bags, carpets, even furniture. Look for baskets of all shapes and sizes in country markets, much less expensive than in the souvenir shops, because people are buying them for everyday use. Woodwork has always been a local speciality, from furniture to carved figurines.

After the cork harvest has been turned into millions of corks for wine bottles, the odds and ends finish up in the hands of artisans, who carve miniature sculptures and assorted knick-knacks. Even the debris isn't wasted, but compressed into place mats and wine coolers.

Gourmet Gifts

Finally, an easy choice for a gift or souvenir: take home a bottle of Port or Madeira, or one of the local spirits: *medronho*, distilled from the arbutus berry; *amêndoa amarga*, an almond liqueur, or the honey-flavoured brandy called *brandymel*.

77

Dining Out

Restaurants in Portugal are modest, friendly places. Waiters are down-to-earth and helpful, unless they're coping with the lunchtime rush in Lisbon or next to an Algarve beach. The food is wholesome and abundant, with an emphasis on fresh fish and shellfish, although meat-eaters are not deprived.

Aside from standard restaurants (*restaurante*), meals can be had in a less formal setting at a *tasca* (tavern), a *churrasqueira* specializing in charcoal-grilled food, a *casa de pasto* (an economical eatery usually offering a set menu) or a *marisqueira* (with the emphasis on seafood).

Meal times follow general European patterns, earlier than in neighbouring Spain. Lunch can be served at any time from 12.30 to 2.30 p.m., and dinner from 7.30 to 9.30 p.m. Restaurants are officially rated in four categories: luxury, 1st, 2nd and 3rd class, but these reflect the facilities and prices, *not* the quality of the food. Menus are generally posted outside, and may include an *ementa turística*, a fixed price economy menu that's not just for tourists. A word of warning: nothing is free. The appetizers that appear on your table unordered (olives, cheese, paté) are charged by the item, depending on what you eat.

Breakfast

For the Portuguese, breakfast is inconsequential—coffee, toast or rolls, butter and jam. Incidentally, the delicious bread looks and tastes home-made. Some hotels lay on a big breakfast buffet for their guests, with everything from cornflakes to omelettes.

Lunch and Dinner

Both main meals are traditionally multi-course affairs. The proceedings often start with a filling soup such as *caldo verde* (green soup), a thick broth of shredded kale, potato purée and perhaps a chunk of sausage. *Sopa à Portuguesa* is similar but with sundry other vegetables. *Gaspacho* is the local interpretation of Andalusia's "liquid salad", a cold soup of tomatoes, cucumbers and peppers.

Fish and Shellfish

The atmosphere means a lot, so if you're on a beach or quayside the *sardinhas assadas* (grilled sardines) and a salad can make a memorable lunch. Much bigger than the ones packed in a can, the sardines are at their best from June to September, nicely corresponding to the holiday season. Rich in calcium, protein and low-cholesterol oils, they are good for you, as well.

Larger fish such as sole, mullet and bream are also grilled, or in some recipes boiled. Tuna *(atum)* and swordfish are sliced into steaks and grilled, or cooked in tasty casseroles. Swordfish is *peixe espadarte* or *peixe agulha*, not to be confused with *peixe espada* (scabbard fish), a thin, sinister-looking giant so long it has to be folded up to fit in the fishermen's trays.

Seafood restaurants usually have the latest trophies on display, so you can point to whatever you fancy. *Amêijoas na cataplana* is an Algarve speciality, steamed baby clams with sausage, ham, onion, tomato, garlic, paprika and white wine, served in the pan used to cook them.

Meat Courses

Pork and lamb are plentiful, and not just the main cuts. Heads, tails and all sorts of offal turn up in traditional dishes. Tripe is such an old favourite in Oporto that the rest of Portugal calls its people *tripeiros* ("tripe-eaters"). *Feijoada* is a stew of white beans and cabbage with sausage, bacon and pork bits, a restrained version of Brazil's national dish.

Frango—chicken—is popular, whether roasted on a spit, barbecued or fried. Spiced up with *piri-piri* (hot chilli), it's a reminder of Portugal's former African possessions, just as curries recall the colonies in India. *Cabrito* means kid, or young goat. *Cabrito estufado* is a stew of kid and onions, tomatoes, potatoes and peas, and *cabrito assado* is baked kid, perhaps with a wine sauce.

Some restaurants, especially in the *pousadas,* specialize in game: venison, quail, partridge, pheasant and wild boar.

BACALHAU

There's no accounting for taste. Fine fresh fish is landed every day at a hundred ports, but the nearest thing to a national dish is *bacalhau*, dried, salted cod which comes in sheets as hard as a board from Norway and other northern seas. After soaking in many changes of water, it can be dressed up in hundreds of ways and turns up everywhere from little local restaurants to top-grade hotels, and it can be the most expensive item on the menu. Portuguese palates relish the strong flavour; foreigners may find it an acquired taste.

Happy Endings

Portuguese desserts are so sweet they probably set some sort of record. Almost every village has its local speciality, if only at festivals—cakes, candies, puddings and pastries always based on the favourite local ingredients—sugar, eggs, almonds and figs. Occasionally chocolate, cinnamon, orange or candied pumpkin add to the flavour.

An old Bolshevik is inexplicably honoured in a rich dessert called *pudim Molotov*, involving meringue and caramel sauce. Standard items in many restaurants are *pudim* (caramel custard) and *arroz doce*, sweetened rice sprinkled with cinnamon. Fresh fruit is usually an option: *laranjas* (oranges), *ananás* (pineapple), bananas, figs or strawberries, according to season.

If cheese is offered, look for *Serra da Estrela*, a rich ewe's milk cheese still made by traditional methods. Light, creamy *queijo fresco* is sometimes served as an appetizer.

Drinks

The Portuguese word *garrafa* means bottle, not carafe. So if you want a carafe of the house wine, ask for *um frasco*. Other than that, all you have to know is *tinto* (red), *branco* (white) and maybe *rosé*. *Vinho verde*, literally "green wine", is the fresh, tart, slightly sparkling wine from northern Portugal. In this case, green means young; most is white, but there is a red version called *vinho verde tinto* (red green wine).

Though the house wines are usually drinkable, and may be excellent, it would be a pity not to try some more distinguished regional varieties, especially if you are travelling round the country. From north of Coimbra, *Bairrada* wines are reliable and full of character. The *Dão* region near Viseu produces smooth, pleasant reds; the best *Dão Reservas* keep for many years. South of Lisbon, some fine dry table wines come from the Arrábida Peninsula, as well as sweet Moscatel de Setúbal from muscat grapes.

The Portuguese like a dry white Port or a dry Madeira as an apéritif. Red and tawny Ports and sweeter Madeiras are the time-honoured way of finishing dinner.

The local beers are refreshing on a hot day. Or you can choose mineral water, fruit juice or the usual international soft drinks.

After lunch or dinner the locals usually order a *bica*, a small cup of black espresso. A *bica* with a little milk in it is called a *garoto*. If you prefer a full-sized white coffee ask for a *galão*; it comes in a tall glass. Tea *(chá)* is also popular—after all, it was the Portuguese who first brought it in quantity to Europe.

Sports

The emphasis is naturally on watersports in summer, and golf and tennis at almost any time. The Algarve is dedicated to leisure, of course, but old-established and newer resorts up and down the west coast have some excellent facilities too. Inland, spring is the perfect season for walking in the Peneda-Gerês national park and the Serra da Estrela mountains.

Water Sports

Atlantic waves and tides mean that the sea and the beaches are generally cleaner in Portugal than along most Mediterranean coasts, though average water temperatures are a bit cooler. Almost all the Algarve beaches have been awarded European blue flags of distinction—more than half of all the beaches so honoured in Portugal. They start at Odeceixe on the southwest coast and run all the way east to Monte Gordo, the endless sandy stretch near the Spanish border. The cliff-backed coves of the west are more spectacular, but the ocean is warmer and swimming is safer for children on the eastern part of the coast.

Surfers gravitate to the more exposed west coast. Expert windsurfers also revel in the challenging conditions there, while the Algarve lagoons sheltered by offshore sandbars are ideal for beginners. Most resorts have boards for hire and instructors on call.

Scuba diving offers dramatic possibilities, particularly among the underwater caves and rock formations of the western Algarve. Equipment and instruction are available at many resorts.

If you want to make your own waves, there's water-skiing at most larger Algarve resorts; the sea is dependably calm in the lagoons. And if you don't mind the nasty looks you'll get, you can rent a jet ski after taking a brief instruction course, and use it in designated areas at some of the long beaches. Renting a dinghy or catamaran is no problem at the bigger resorts; for larger yachts, crewed or bareboat, try the main marinas such as Vilamoura.

Fishing

The Portuguese love fishing; you'll see them perched on every possible rock and pier, or casting 81

Quinta do Lago offers challenging courses for players of all levels.

lines into the lakes and rivers. There's nothing to stop you joining in, as long as you don't get in their way, but note that a permit is needed for freshwater fishing—ask at tourist offices.

Deep-sea fishing expeditions going after swordfish, marlin or shark are offered at the quayside at ports such as Sesimbra, Setúbal, Portimão and at the Vilamoura marina.

Golf, Anyone?

A handful of clubs can be found near Lisbon and along the west coast, but it's the Algarve which is a magnet for Europe's golfers. They can play all year round, on courses landscaped by famous designers in the varied settings of sand dunes, rolling hills and pine woods. The cliff-top holes can take your breath away, though you may pay for the view by driving a ball into the ocean.

Some of the finest championship courses are attached to the major resort complexes, such as Vale do Lobo, Quinta do Lago and Vilamoura. Visitors staying in hotels, apartments or villas in these resorts thus have easy access to the links, sometimes as part of a package deal. Other hotels advertise specially reduced green fees at nearby clubs. You may need a handicap certificate.

Tennis, Too

More and more tennis players are coming to the Algarve to perfect their game, and some well-known tennis personalities have lent their names to specially designed tennis centres offering intensive coaching. Floodlighting extends the hours of play into the cooler evening. Those who take the game less seriously will find many hotels with courts in all parts of Portugal. At larger resorts, there may be equipment for rent and perhaps optional tuition.

Horse Riding

The scenery, the climate and a long tradition attract all who love horses, all year round. There are famous and fashionable equestrian clubs near Lisbon, and some of the country estates which take paying guests keep horses for them to ride.

Most of the Algarve's stables are along the coast starting west of Faro, where the terrain becomes more dramatic. Activities range from pony rides for children to show-jumping advice for experienced riders, and treks along the beaches or through the pine forests.

Spectator Sports

Almost a national religion, football (meaning soccer) stirs up the usually impassive Portuguese like nothing else. When the two Lisbon teams, Benfica and Sporting, or FC Porto are playing the fans pack the stadiums and fill the bars to watch the match on TV. The season runs from September to May.

Bullfighting is an ancient tradition, but unlike a Spanish bullfight, the object of the Portuguese *tourada* is not to kill the bull. Or at least not as part of the spectacle—poor performers may be despatched offstage afterwards. A fight in the old Portuguese style begins with a *cavaleiro* in 18th-century costume, mounted on an exquisitely trained horse, stabbing darts into the bull's shoulders. Next to appear are eight bullfighters on foot, the *forcados*, who have to subdue the bull with their bare hands. In other fights, one man on foot faces the bull, equipped only with his cape, before the eight *forcados* take over.

The home of bullfighting in Portugal is the Ribatejo, northeast of Lisbon. From Easter to October, *touradas* are held in the towns of the region such as Santarém and Vila Franca de Xira, where the bulls are sometimes run through the streets first. Bullfighting is not a tradition in the Algarve, but it has been introduced for the tourist trade, with night performances to escape the summer heat. Elsewhere they start at 5 p.m.

83

The Hard Facts

Airports

Lisbon International Airport is sometimes called Portela, the name of the suburb where it's located, about 5 km (3 miles) north of the city. There's a frequent bus service to the centre, and Cais do Sodré station.

Oporto's Francisco Sá Carneiro Airport is 18 km (11 miles) north of the centre. Buses run to the main railway station in the centre.

Faro International Airport, 5 km (3 miles) west of the city, sees a huge volume of traffic in summer, much less at other times. Buses run to the centre but most arrivals pick up rental cars or are met by tour company representatives and taken to their hotels or villas.

All three major airports have the usual amenities—free baggage trolleys, information desk, car hire counters, bars, restaurants, shops, currency exchange and taxis.

Climate

Summers are hot and dry, especially in the interior and the south, though sea breezes temper the heat on the beaches. The west coast tends to be windier, with some chance of rain in the north. Spring is an ideal time for touring, with wild flowers blooming and no crowds. September and October are still hot enough for a beach holiday on the Algarve, where in winter there's only a one-in-three chance of a rainy day—good odds for golfers and tennis players. The mountains in the north see some winter snow, with frequent rain on the north and west coasts.

Communications

The postal service works, although it can be slow; your postcards may arrive after you get home. Stamps *(selos)* are sold at the post office *(correios)* and at many of the shops which sell postcards.

Telephone calls from hotel rooms are convenient but costly, as most hotels add high surcharges. Public telephones are mostly card-operated. Phone cards are sold at news-stands and post offices. You can also make calls at post offices, where you talk first and pay later. Some privately operated telephone offices offer similar facilities. To make an international call, dial 00, the country code (1 for US, 44 for UK), area code and local number. Portugal's country code is 351.

Faxes can be sent and received at many hotels. This service is also available at telephone service bureaux.

Complaints

If you have a grievance in a hotel or restaurant, ask to see whoever is in charge and calmly explain your problem. If it isn't satisfactorily solved, ask for the *livro de reclamações*, the official complaint book. This may speed a solution, for the manager would be reluctant to have a complaint forwarded to the tourism authorities.

Customs

Passengers from non-EU countries aged 17 years or over can bring in the following, duty-free:
– 200 cigarettes or 50 cigars
– 1 litre of spirits
– 2 litres of wine
– 50 g perfume
– 250 ml eau de toilette.
Passengers from other EU countries can bring much larger quantities of tax-*paid* goods:
– 800 cigarettes or 200 cigars
– 90 litres wine
– 110 litres beer
– No restrictions on perfumes.
There are no limits on the amount of euros or foreign currency in cash or travellers cheques you can import. Leaving, the limit is the equivalent of 5,000 euros in foreign currency.

Driving

Modern highways connect most major cities; long stretches of *auto-estrada* (motorway) include toll sections. Country roads may be rough and tortuous. Rules are typical of western Europe: drive on the right, overtake on the left, wear seat belts, don't drink and drive. Unless otherwise marked, the speed limits are 120 kph (75 mph) on motorways, 90 kph (56 mph) on other highways, and 60 kph (37 mph) in built-up areas. Local driving standards have improved, but drivers tend to ignore speed limits and still take hair-raising risks. Beware, too, of farm tractors, animals and unlit vehicles at night.

Parking is difficult in town centres. Some have installed parking meters, some use a pay-and-display method.

Renting a car is straightforward, with local and international companies competing at the airports and resorts. The differences in tariffs tend to be small. Unless you pay with a major credit card you'll have to put down a large deposit.

Emergencies

For police, fire or ambulance service (*polícia, bombeiros, ambulância*), the all-purpose emergency number is 112. In more complex cases, contact your consulate.

Police wearing armbands marked "CD" (local corps) are there to help visitors; they probably have some knowledge of foreign languages. Highway patrols are run by the Guarda Nacional Republicana (GNR), often patrolling in pairs on motorcycles.

Etiquette

Portuguese people are quietly courteous, even formal, shaking hands whenever meeting and taking leave. It's polite to say *"Bom dia"* when you enter a shop or before asking for help.

Visitors from countries where smokers have been ostracized may be surprised to find that Portugal still smokes up a storm—in restaurants, cafés, offices, hotel lobbies and in the street. But smoking is prohibited on buses and in cinemas and theatres.

Luxury hotels and top restaurants encourage a touch of formality, and businesspeople dress soberly. In holiday areas dress is casual, but swimsuits are inappropriate in towns, and if you visit a church it's only proper to dress respectably.

Formalities

Visitors from most countries require only a valid passport, with no visa, to enter Portugal for stays of up to 90 days. National identity cards are sufficient for most European nationals.

Health

The main thing to worry about is an overdose of sun or wine. Use a sunscreen with a high protection factor, stay in the shade during the middle of the day, wear a hat and shirt when possible. For small problems—like mosquito bites or queasy stomach—consult any pharmacy. Chemists *(farmácias)* are open during normal business hours; after hours a duty chemist *(farmácia de serviço)* stays open late. The address is found in local newspapers or by the door of any other pharmacy.

For more serious ailments or injuries, ask at your hotel or the tourist office for a list of English-speaking doctors, or go to the nearest hospital. Portugal has reciprocal health agreements with most European countries. Visitors with UK passports are entitled to free in-patient treatment in officially designated hospitals; other EU nationals must present form E111.

If you take prescription medicines, it's wise to pack all you need; it may not be easy to track down the Portuguese equivalent in the correct dosage.

Holidays and Festivals

January 1	New Year's Day
April 25	National Day
May 1	Labour Day
June 10	Portugal (or Camões) Day

August 15	Assumption
October 5	Republic Day
November 1	All Saints' Day
December 1	Restoration Day (Independence)
December 8	Immaculate Conception
December 25	Christmas

Moveable: Shrove Tuesday, Good Friday and Corpus Christi. In addition, every town celebrates its own saint's day with everything from religious processions to fireworks.

Language

Close to 200 million people speak Portuguese, most of them in former possessions such as Brazil and Mozambique. Brazil has its own eccentricities in spelling and pronunciation, but they pose no problem for the millions of Portuguese addicted to the Brazilian soap operas on television.

Wherever tourists gather, English and German are widely understood, and many Portuguese speak French. If you know Spanish, you'll probably be able to read the signs, and even the newspapers, although you won't understand the spoken tongue. But don't try speaking in Spanish, even to say "thank you", if you want to avoid giving offence.

Media

Leading European newspapers arrive in the big cities and major holiday centres on the day of publication or the day after, and there's a range of international magazines on sale.

Portugal's four television channels rarely carry anything of interest to foreigners, although they do show some films in the original language with Portuguese subtitles. In some areas, Spanish TV can also be seen. Many hotels have satellite channels (in English, French, German, Italian and other languages) so you can generally watch the news on BBC World, Sky or CNN. Some local stations schedule TV and radio programmes in English and French aimed at tourists.

Money

Portugal has adopted the euro, divided into 100 cents. Coins: 1, 2, 5, 10, 20 and 50 cents, 1 and 2 euros; banknotes: 5, 10, 20, 50, 100, 200 and 500 euros..

Travellers cheques can be cashed at banks and exchange bureaux *(câmbio)*, and there are 24-hour automatic cash machines which dispense euros billed to your home bank or credit card, provided you remember your personal identification number (PIN).

Opening Hours

Banks open Monday to Friday, 8.30 a.m.–3 p.m. Post offices (CTT or Correios) open Monday 87 to Friday from 8.30 or 9 a.m. to 6 or 6.30 p.m.; some close for lunch. City centre offices also operate Saturday mornings until 12.30 p.m.

Shops open Monday to Friday 9 a.m. to 1 p.m. and 3 to 7 p.m., and on Saturdays from 9 a.m. to 1 p.m. Big shopping centres usually stay open later, some until 10 or 11 p.m., and most open on Sundays.

Museums generally open every day except Mondays and public holidays, from 10 a.m. to 5 p.m. Some close from 12 or 12.30 p.m. to 2 or 2.30 p.m.

Photography and Video

All the popular types of film are available at photo shops, newsstands and souvenir shops; colour print film is processed in 24 hours or less. Transparency (slide) film is best taken back to your home country for processing.

Standard varieties of video tape are available. Note that pre-recorded tape is incompatible with US systems.

Public Transport

Within the big cities, buses are frequent and fares are reasonable. Lisbon also has colourful trams, and a fast, modern Metro (underground railway).

Buses, most of them comfortable, link all the main cities and towns. Timetables are posted at tourist offices and bus stations. Modern air-conditioned coaches do the long-distance journeys.

Much of the country is served by Portuguese Railways (CP), though some of the stations are far away from town centres. There are reduced fares for children aged 4–11 and a Senior Citizen rate for people over 65, and various money-saving fares valid for unlimited travel. Charges are higher on the high speed (*Rápido*) and intercity services.

In all main towns and resorts, taxis are available, waiting at ranks and hotels. They can also be summoned by telephone. They should have meters, and should switch them on. In rural areas, there are flat rates for standard journeys; it's prudent to agree on the fare in advance.

Religion

The overwhelming majority of Portuguese are Roman Catholics. Although church attendance is declining, it is still high, and the population is swept up by the many religious festivals that punctuate the year.

Foreign visitors are catered for in larger resorts, where Catholic and Protestant services in English and other languages are announced on the bulletin boards of tourist offices and hotels. In Lisbon, Anglican services are held at St George's Church in the Estrela district. You can find out about the services of other denominations and religions from local tourist offices or the concierge desks of large hotels.

Safety

Car rental companies strongly advise their customers to close windows and lock all doors, and to have nothing of value on view. They also recommend parking in secure car parks, especially at night, and to leave nothing in the vehicle, visible or hidden. The risk of car theft, or break-ins, is greatest at beaches and other spots where cars may be left for long periods.

Street crime is a fact of life in big cities, so avoid being alone at night in dark and less-frequented areas. It's wise to keep valuables and most of your cash in safe deposit boxes; some hotels and apartment complexes have them in the rooms.

Time

Portugal is on the same westerly longitude as Ireland and, unlike most other west European countries, sticks to GMT, or GMT + 1 from April to October. So the time is the same as in Britain and Ireland, one hour behind Spain.

Tipping

Hotel and restaurant bills generally include a service charge, but it's usual to leave a small tip as well. For service personnel, hairdressers and taxi drivers, 10 per cent is a reasonable tip. Hotel porters expect at least 1 euro for carrying bags.

Toilets

In cities or at tourist sites look for the signs *WC Senhoras* (ladies) and *WC Homens* (men). Otherwise, your best bet is the nearest hotel, restaurant or café (where you should order at least a soft drink or coffee).

Tourist Information

Practically every town has a tourist information office (*posto do turismo*), generally staffed by helpful people who speak several languages, and English in particular. Maps and leaflets are available and the office can usually help with accommodation.

www.portugal.org
www.icep.pt

Voltage

Electric current is 220 volts AC, 50 Hz, using round pins as elsewhere on the Continent. American appliances require transformers and plug adapters.

Water

Tap water is officially safe to drink, but may taste chlorinated. Many people prefer bottled mineral water.

89

AROUND LISBON

PORTO

0   200 m

0   200 yd

N

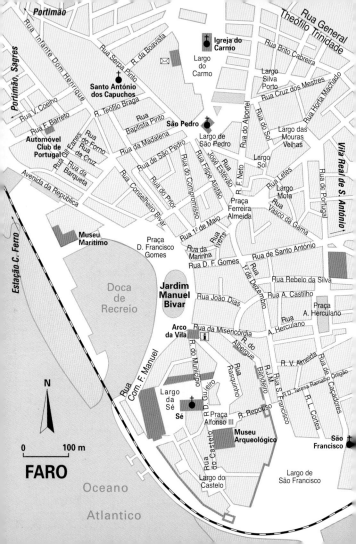

Portimão

Rua General Theófilo Trinidade

Rua Serpa Pinto

R. da Boavista

Rua Infante Dom Henrique

Portimão, Sagres

✝ Igreja do Carmo

Rua Brito Cabreira

Largo do Carmo

Rua Teófilo Braga

Santo António dos Capuchos

Largo Silva Porto

Rua Cruz dos Mestres

Rua Horta Machado

Rua V. Coelho

Rua F. Barreto

Rua Baptista Pinto

São Pedro ✝

Rua da Madalena

Largo de São Pedro

Rua do Alportel

Rua do Sol

Largo das Mouras Velhas

Vila Real de S. António

Automóvel Club de Portugal

Rua do Forno

Rua da Cruz

Rua de São Pedro

Rua do Compromisso

Rua Filipe Alistão

Rua José Estevão

Largo Sol

R. F. Neto

Rua Lethes

Rua de Portugal

Rua Eanes

Rua Gil

Rua da Barqueta

Rua Conselheiro Bivar

Rua do Prior

Praça Ferreira Almeida

Largo Mota

Avenida da República

Rua 1º de Maio

Rua Irens

Rua Vasco da Gama

Museu Marítimo

Praça D. Francisco Gomes

Rua da Marinha

Rua D. F. Gomes

Rua de Santo António

Rua 1º de Dezembro

Rua Rebelo da Silva

Doca de Recreio

Jardim Manuel Bivar

Rua João Dias

Rua A. Castilho

Praça A. Herculano

Estação C. Ferro

Arco da Vila ℹ

Rua da Misericórdia

R. do Albergue

A. Herculano

Rua

R. V. Almeida

Rua Com. F. Manuel

R. do Município

Rua Rasquinho

R.J.M. Bandeiro

R. de Fonte Ramalho Ortigão

R. J. M. Bandeiro

Largo da Sé

R. D. Guieiro

R. Repouso

R. São Francisco

Sé ✝

Praça Alfonso III

Museu Arqueológico

R. L. Cortes

R.D. Teresa Ramalho Ortigão

São Francisco ✝

Rua do Castelo

N

Largo do Castelo

Largo de São Francisco

0   100 m

FARO

Oceano

Atlantico

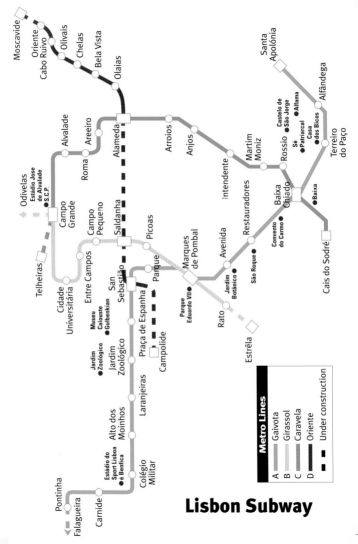

Lisbon Subway

Moscavide
Oriente
Cabo Ruivo
Olivais
Chelas
Bela Vista
Olaias

Santa Apolónia
Alfândega
Terreiro do Paço

Alvalade
Areeiro
Alameda
Arroios
Anjos

Castelo de São Jorge
Alfama
Rossio
Sé
Patriarcal
Casa dos Bicos

Odivelas
Estádio José de Alvalade S.C.P.
Roma
Martim Moniz
Baixa

Campo Grande
Campo Pequeno
Saldanha
Picoas
Intendente
Restauradores
Baixa/Chiado

Telheiras
Cidade Universitária
Entre Campos
Parque
Marquês de Pombal
Avenida
Convento do Carmo
São Roque
Cais do Sodré

Museu Calouste Gulbenkian
San Sebastião
Parque Eduardo VII
Jardim Botânico
Rato

Praça de Espanha
Campolide
Estrêla

Jardim Zoológico
Jardim Zoológico

Laranjeiras
Alto dos Moinhos
Colégio Militar

Pontinha
Falagueira
Carnide
Estádio do Sport Lisboa e Benfica

Metro Lines

A Gaivota
B Girassol
C Caravela
D Oriente
    Under construction

INDEX

INDEX (continued)

GENERAL EDITOR
  Barbara Ender-Jones
EDITORS
  Mark Little
  Mark Harding
LAYOUT
  Luc Malherbe
PHOTO CREDITS
  Agnès Bouteville: pp. 1, 32;
  Hémisphères: pp. 2, 5, 21,
  23, 38–39, 43, 61, 63, 72;
  Paul Bernhardt: pp. 8, 26, 48,
  51, 58, 82;
  Jo Holz: pp. 6–7, 13, 54–55;
  VISA/Louvet: p. 16;
  Claude Huber: p. 69
MAPS
  Elsner & Schichor;
  Huber Kartographie;
  JPM Publications

Copyright © 2002
by JPM Publications S.A.
12, avenue William-Fraisse,
1006 Lausanne, Switzerland
information@jpmguides.com
www.jpmguides.com/

Printed in Switzerland
Weber/Bienne (CTP) — 02/06/02